A Field
Kingdom Education

Insights from Comenius School for Creative Leadership

SANDY WOODS et al

MorningStar Publications

A Field Guide for Kingdom Education:
Insights from the Comenius School for Creative Leadership
By Sandy Woods et al

©2020 1st Printing

MorningStar Ministries, Fort Mill, SC. All rights reserved.

Distributed by MorningStar Publications, Inc.,
a division of MorningStar Fellowship Church
375 Star Light Drive, Fort Mill, Sc 29715

www.MorningStarMinistries.org
1-800-542-0278

Cover design: Emily Laney
Layout design: Carlie McKinley
Editor: Sarah Godwin

ISBN: 978-1-60708-675-8

Table of Contents

ENDORSEMENTS

This has to at least be one of the most comprehensive books available about both the purpose and operational nature of kingdom schooling. Descriptions of practical, even Holy Spirit guided applications abound in this magnificent publication. A recurring main theme relates to how to embed academics and classroom dynamics within a culture of honor such that the personalized imago Dei nature of students, teachers, and parents flourish as God intends. This book should be recognized as a valuable reference for all schools intentionally Christian in nature!

William F. Cox, Jr., PhD (Professor - retired)
Chair-Christian School Program, School of Education, Regent University

Having walked closely as a sister-school to CSCL and Sandy Woods, I heartily endorse this book and this school. CSCL is a greenhouse in kingdom education to train up students to be passionate believers and society influencers. They have a spirit of innovation and joy that is unmatchable! I have gleaned so much through the years for our Kansas City school as well.

Lauren Fraser
Principal Emeritus
The Daniel Academy, Kansas City MO

Education everywhere is in a state of flux. Everyone is rethinking how to educate the next generation of leaders. Enter: **A Field Guide for Kingdom Education**—*a timely book for Christian parents and educators everywhere exploring the role of the Holy Spirit in educating our children. Some books discuss theory and* *philosophy, but this one features practical insights and wisdom from the CSCL teachers in the trenches. At the heart of this book are stories bursting with Holy Spirit-inspired principles that can be incorporated into our home learning and school environments at this hour. Read this book! Highly recommended!*

Robert Rummage
Pastor of Prayer and Intercession
Morningstar Fellowship Church, Fort Mill, SC

Kingdom education is not an endeavor for the faint-hearted Christian. Kingdom educators are called to partner with parents to raise up a generation that are "high-impact lovers of God who are simultaneously the bride of Christ and the army of God." The practical application of kingdom principles found in **A Field Guide for Kingdom Education: Insights from the Comenius School for Creative Leadership** *are treasures for any parent or kingdom educator that seeks to raise up a holy remnant that is grounded firmly in their relationship with God, identity in Christ, and divine destiny. The wisdom and practical guidance found in these pages is truly priceless and will help kingdom educators all over the world achieve the purpose of kingdom education!*

Amy Davies, MA, Ed.S.
Education Specialist
Ph.D. student at Regent University

This book is so needed in Christian education today, because it highlights what can happen when the administration, teachers, and students are focused on bringing God's kingdom into the classroom. Sandy and the other teachers offer compelling real-life stories of how students grow in their faith when trained and encouraged to hear God and to use their unique spiritual gifts. Having served as the Headmaster of three Christian schools, I can attest to the life-changing value of this book for educators. You will be amazed at the potential of kingdom education to empower and equip K-12 students—to be all God has called them to be—spiritually, academically, and as children of God.

Homer Allen
A Firm Foundation, President

This field guide for kingdom educators is a welcomed resource for teachers and administrators today. CSCL and principal Sandy Woods share twenty plus years of practical experience in teaching students to hear God's voice, pray for the sick, and excel in their God-given strengths, all during a typical school day.

Josh and Ginger Hallmark
Directors
The Oaks School, Auburn, AL

The Comenius School for Creative Leadership (CSCL) was revolutionary from its founding. It was named after John Amos Comenius who is considered "the father of modern education," who is not only the greatest genius to ever work in the field of education, but remains its most revolutionary thinker. Having applied some of the basics of his vision from the founding of CSCL, the impact was immediate and dramatic. The students, love for school, and love of learning quickly soared beyond what we had witnessed before. **A Field Guide for Kingdom Education** *is written by some of our staff and teachers who have been on this journey to see the love of knowledge and love for the truth become again the glorious adventure it should be.*

Rick Joyner
Founder and Executive Director
MorningStar Ministries

INTRODUCTION

TRAIN TO REIGN

by Joe Chamberlin

"For those who have their faculties trained by practice to distinguish good from evil" (Hebrews 5:14).

This book addresses the need for an educational field training manual. We want to show how the kingdom of God is expressed in a school setting, and share our experience with other educators who are dedicated to equipping students to fight the good fight.

The U.S. Army published a manual in 1966 on *Unconventional Warfare Devices and Techniques.* The preface states that in order for an item to be included in the manual, the device is first tested for effectiveness, reliability, and safety. Detailed instructions were given that must be followed precisely to assure proper functioning of these devices.

Warfare is serious business, and not pretty or merely intellectual. Military training requires understanding *and* application. Trainees are required to demonstrate their proficiency. Consequences of achievement or failure to perform are real and significant. Do we take education that seriously?

I. Does our concept of education prepare students for the challenges ahead?

Because of the internet and social media, this generation is intensely aware of moral conflict, political division, civil strife, and economic inequality. They are in a continual battle for their hearts and minds.

Many educators, bound by legalism and inclusivity, avoid conflict as much as possible. Much of modern education consists of dispensing information and then evaluating whether that dispensed information has been understood, at least temporarily. There is little application and even less consideration of personal responsibility. "No child left behind" often means promotion without merit. The consequences of this approach are devastating.

According to a recent Pentagon estimate, only 25% of American youth are eligible to join the military. The rest are disqualified due to drug use, obesity, illiteracy, mental health problems, and criminal records. About 20% of our youth do not graduate high school. Of those with a diploma, 20% are functionally illiterate. Over 50% cannot pass math and science competency exams implemented by Common Core standards. This is after an average of $150,000 of taxpayer money has been invested in twelve years of "education."

Even the general public realizes that the current system has failed to be effective, reliable, or safe. Since the Supreme Court took the Bible out of public schools in 1948, humanism has taken control of the public school system. Because our American culture has degenerated into mostly shallow, rocky, and thorny soil, it is not surprising to see the sad effect on our youth.

II. What has happened to "train up a child in the way he should go?"

As followers of Christ, we do take education seriously. The challenges our students face are much bigger than an elevated GPA or an SAT score that will get them into university. Some studies indicate only 10% of self-identified Christian youth maintain a walk with God while in college. Even in their high school years, most of these young minds have been constantly bombarded with the humanistic world view.

Consider the three basic steps of training: demonstrate the process, practice the process with the trainee, and then evaluate the trainee as they complete the process on their own. As parents and teachers, these three issues have to be front and center in a Spirit-filled environment: demonstrate the character of Christ, reinforce godly attitudes and behavior, and then release our students to experience the kingdom of God on a daily basis.

The stories and chapters of this book are designed to give specific examples of how the kingdom of God can be expressed in the classroom. The emphasis is letting the Spirit of God direct each class, lesson by lesson, moment by moment. We are constantly amazed by the creative, life-changing process that we are privileged to share.

III. How does someone become qualified to be a trainer? What is a suitable training environment?

These are good questions to present to the Superintendent of our souls. Many of the qualifications of a Christian leader are given in I and II Timothy. God has poured into each of the staff at our school our own series of mentors and life experiences. The discernment and wisdom so lacking in many schools is evident here. We ourselves have been trained by many years of practice to discern good from evil. It is not a great intellect or a college degree that qualifies someone to teach at a school like CSCL. The teachers here have a calling on their life, and the Spirit has confirmed that calling day by day.

Is the vision of your school bigger than academics? Are the directors of your school submitting their administrative decisions to God's direction? Yes, we all are aware that a school is often held accountable like a business—there are standards for legalities, finances, and facilities. But a Christian school is a family business, and family must come before business. Does a mother count the hours taking care of a sick child? Does a father begrudge the money to feed and clothe his children? The most important question to evaluate the effectiveness of a school is, "Do the students know they are loved?"

Sure, we need classrooms, technology, gymnasiums, and cafeterias. But it is very possible to build a facility or an organization and have no awareness of the presence of God. We do not want to build on sand, but on the Solid Rock. Christ promised that if we seek first the kingdom of God, all these things shall be added to us, and the fruit of our labor would endure. At CSCL, academics and athletics take second and third priority. Our first priority is to experience in our classrooms the joy, peace, and righteousness of the kingdom of God. King Jesus is our Teacher, and He anoints our teaching.

IV. Who are we training?

We are not a school that just scatters seed everywhere hoping some will grow. A school like CSCL is cultivating good soil. Good soil consists of students who have the family support to follow Christ, who have a sense of God's destiny on their lives, and who have a teachable spirit.

Each student who applies to CSCL must be accountable to a responsible adult who is a committed follower of Christ. Each student is asked to state why they want to attend our school and be able to speak to their current relationship with God. Each student is asked to sign a code of conduct, which has been formulated with the help of their classmates.

Even after admittance, each student is accepted on a probationary status to see if their character and performance meet the requirements for continued enrollment. If a student is struggling in some area, each disciplinary decision is first covered in prayer, asking for God's wisdom and direction. Not every student is ready for a Spirit-led school experience. Those who are ready will enjoy their preparation for great adventures. It is God's wisdom that provides the detailed instructions to cultivate the good soil.

V. Are there models to follow in training this generation?

The millennial generation faces great technical, social, and spiritual challenges. We are here to raise up Christian leaders to meet these challenges. We are trainers, working with a crew of trainers, investing our lives in the righteous leadership of the future. We are following the advice that Paul gave to Timothy, **"What you have heard from me in the presence of many witnesses entrust to faithful men, who will be able to teach others also" (II Timothy 2:2 ESV).**

The following chapters contain examples of life-lesson experiences by the staff at the Comenius School for Creative Leadership. We earnestly desire **"the Great Shepherd of** the sheep . . . equip you with everything good that you may do His will, working in you that which is pleasing in His sight" (Hebrews 13:20-21 ESV).

SECTION I

SCHOOL STRUCTURE, VISION, AND CULTURE

CHAPTER 1

NON-NEGOTIABLES FOR LEADERS (DEVELOP YOUR TEAM)

by Sandy Woods

Every school has a team of dedicated staff members whose main goal is to ensure quality education for its students. It is up to the school leader (headmaster, principal, top administrator) to build that team, encourage and provide opportunities for improvement, and give direction as the Holy Spirit leads.

It is imperative that the faculty understand four key elements to develop the culture in a kingdom school. I call these the "non-negotiables" that allow kingdom teachers and their students to flourish.

1. Understand the mission

2. Set the atmosphere

3. Choose liberty

4. Protect the children

Understand the Mission

Schools have mission statements, but does every member understand it? Has each one adopted it? Is the mission statement evident in and out of the classroom? At CSCL, the staff has its own mission statement which fits the call of those who teach and work at CSCL:

CSCL Staff Mission Statement – We equip students to be secure in their relationship with the Lord and confident in who they are, in order that they are free to take risks, seek continual personal growth, and are prepared to pursue "the way they should go" with excellence.

The importance of each staff member knowing their mission cannot be emphasized enough. The mission statement outlines the communal purpose of each member. One of the first things the CSCL staff does at the beginning of the school year is review our mission. Going over "what we do" energizes each teacher and provides direction and focus. New staff members know exactly what they are tasked with, and returning teachers are reminded of their job's value.

We devote an entire morning to celebrate the importance of each teacher's calling. The mission statement is dissected as seasoned staff members share stories of how each component has benefited them, how the values work in students at school, and how current teachers can use these guiding principles in their day-to-day duties. We share success stories but also tales in which we have fallen short so that all may learn from both our triumphs and our failures.

Each teacher must not only understand the mission, but the mission must become their own. There have been a few times when staff members have clearly not adopted the CSCL mission. That is not to say that they had a bad or harmful mission, it just wasn't ours. This showed up in their classrooms. One teacher tried to prevent her students from taking risks or experimenting with ideas in her classroom; she preferred to play it safe and stick to her pre-conceived lessons. But playing it safe flies in the face of our purpose in kingdom education, and she was faced with bored children who couldn't wait to leave her classroom. The learning experience was difficult for them and they let their parents know it. I had to confront that teacher with our mission statement and ask her to allow the students to take some risks and apply concepts in different and unfamiliar ways. The dynamics in her classroom improved, but never to the point where the students felt that they had complete freedom to be themselves in her classroom.

> One year, I did not lead the staff through the mission statement because it was printed in the teacher handbook. I assumed they had read and taken it to heart. We began the year by going over school routine, teacher responsibilities, and obligations. That year felt "flat" and some of the staff even mentioned a lack of clear vision during the year. Later in the year, the staff met to dispel any doubts and clear up any misunderstandings. I vowed never again to start without going over our mission statement.

Set the Atmosphere

We are told by visitors that they can tell our school is different the minute they set foot in the door. They tell us that they can discern that the Spirit of the Lord is welcome at CSCL and some have even said, "The Holy Spirit likes it here!" How does this happen?

1. Students are brought to the King

"But Jesus said, 'Let the little children come to Me, and do not forbid them; for of such is the kingdom of heaven'" (Matthew 19:14).

Even though most of our students have been brought up in church, many have never had an encounter with Jesus. Don Mayer, principal of Bethel Christian School in Redding, CA, says that kingdom educators owe their students encounters with the Lord. Not to do so is to fail them. We start each school day with student-led prayer and praise and worship. On the first day of every school year, the first day of the new calendar year, and the last day of school, our students are greeted and led through an amazing prayer tunnel, manned first by staff and eventually by all the students who have walked through it. Everyone is prayed for, blessed, and prophesied over. Throughout the school year, there are numerous opportunities in chapel, in classrooms, and on ministry trips to experience the Lord and His presence. There are times in corporate meetings where the atmosphere is "thick" with the weighty presence of the Lord. During those times, students may become completely silent; at other times, they stand and repent; at still other times, they declare the goodness of the Lord and publicly adore Him.

2. Holy Spirit is Welcome

"For the kingdom of God is not eating and drinking, but righteousness and peace and joy in the Holy Spirit" (Romans 14:17).

"Do not quench the Spirit" (1 Thessalonians 5:19).

Each year, our student body consists of "seasoned" Christians who know their spiritual gifts and practice them as well as other students with varied knowledge of spiritual gifts. Students who are mature in the Lord accept that others are not at their "level." Many are eager for the chance to help others discover their spiritual gifts and begin to use them. It is not uncommon to see students encouraging others to pray, sing, prophesy, or lay hands on someone for healing. Many students have received their prayer language in a corporate chapel when one student used a tongue to pray and others were hungry for that. At times, we practice declarations and each student comes forward and affirms who God is or states an aspect of His character. At other times, students are asked to give a prophetic word or draw a picture for someone.

Care is taken not to quench what the Holy Spirit is doing. If the students are engaged with the Lord, the staff lets them continue. We ask the Lord for discernment to know how to steward what He is doing. Sometimes class time is shortened as we extend corporate morning chapel, and sometimes we continue the chapel time in our individual classrooms to allow the Holy Spirit to keep moving within the smaller class setting. At other times we know that it is time to move on to academics. Although we take care not to end these supernatural times prematurely, we seek to finish them appropriately so that the students are hungry for more.

> Prior to a recent Immersion for Educators* held at CSCL, students in the elementary grades were asked to write or draw a prophetic word for our attendees. Each person received a written word and a separate prophetic drawing. One participant arrived in a shaken state due to upheaval in her family. The written word she received comforted her—a 3rd grader had written that God was with her far above the trouble and the prophetic drawing was of her in the sky high above a rainbow. She knew God had seen her and she was reassured.

3. Emphasize Culture, not Curriculum

This is almost a mantra at CSCL. I tell teachers that they are the curriculum that every student reads. They are released to teach as Holy Spirit leads. Many receive downloads for the day to enhance a lesson or help a certain student. All the teachers are urged to seek Him for direction and anointing. Written plans, textbooks, and curricula are tools, but the Spirit is the true Teacher. Although we use much of the same curriculum that the local public schools use, we are not bound by it. Teachers may divert from it, inject their Christian worldview, teach a Spirit-inspired lesson, etc.

During the first month of school, we set aside time to celebrate our culture. The elementary grades focus on identity; these young students learn about who they are as individuals and what makes them tick. The middle grade students go offsite for team building activities and an overnight camping trip. This fosters unity and builds confidence in who they are. Students in grades eight through twelve spend three days and two nights at two different retreat centers; the boys go to one center and the girls to another. There are teachings on the Father's heart and other topics, worship, activities, and plenty of time for making new friends. New students often testify that they hardly knew anyone before the retreat and after they felt accepted and known. While many students make new friend connections during this time, the main purpose is to introduce them to our culture in a protected environment.

4. Choose Liberty

The main difference between our culture and others is the freedom that is evident at CSCL. The staff is tasked as watchmen of freedom and caretakers who make sure it is promoted and protected. **"Now the Lord is Spirit and where the Spirit of the Lord is, there is liberty. There is liberty to choose to act as wise free people or to**

limit that freedom and the self-governance of others" (II Corinthians 3:17 NASB).

Freedom requires that those who live within the culture are self-controlled and honorable to all. Modeling and teaching this to students is no small feat. This truly is where the staff is the curriculum. We teach the older students that they are held in high esteem by the younger ones who love to imitate them, so they too must take care to use their freedom wisely. One of our core beliefs is that everyone has the right to learn and no one has the right to take that away. Is there a disruption in the classroom? The student causing it will be reminded of this core belief and that his/her freedom cannot be used to prevent others from learning.

After the teaching on the first night at the girls' retreat, several girls went outside to worship on their own. As they sang, others joined them. Several began to pray aloud. A few began to pray in tongues, pacing, and even falling to the ground, unable to get up because of the anointing. This continued for over two hours with most of the girls participating at some point. I received word the next day that the teaching at the boys' camp was particularly intense. When I asked the girls what they were praying for, they had no idea, but when I suggested that it might have been for the boys at their camp, they whole heartedly agreed that was it!

The "no assigned homework" policy is a great example of how freedom works at CSCL. In many schools, homework is given simply because it is a part of school and much of this is pure busywork. However, there are times in which doing extra work is beneficial. At CSCL, students must recognize when it is in their best interest not only to review their school work on a regular basis and study for tests and quizzes, but also to read ahead for the next day's work, practice math problems at home, or delve deeper into a topic that interests them. This develops self-discipline within the student and a responsibility for their own education. Graduates often return to tell us of how well they are doing at college because they had cultivated self-study while at CSCL.

Many visitors have observed that our students handle their freedom very well. In the classroom, they express their opinions candidly and confidently. Teachers may ask students to explain why they believe a certain way, not to shut them down, but to explore themes more in depth. Higher level thinking cannot be stimulated unless students are challenged and encouraged to consider other options and opinions. One of our history teachers will almost always play devil's advocate to motivate students to research a topic they are passionate about.

Liberty is evident in our corporate meeting times and chapel. Students often leave their seats to worship elsewhere in the room, without the distraction of being next to someone. Some raise their hands in praise, others may dance. At times, students may ask if they can share something that is on their heart or a word from the Lord. Recently, one student felt strongly that we should wait on the Lord in silence and the students did just that, breaking it only with a song to the Lord. Later, several students shared what they heard the Lord saying to them for the student body. We realize that everyone has a bad day from time to time, so students are also free not to participate and to sit quietly.

Without the freedom to make a wrong choice, it is impossible to learn self-governance. External controls and fear of punishment put limitations on children to keep them in check, thus they never develop a healthy fear of the Lord or the discipline to monitor themselves. Some of the best lessons learned come after making a mistake. At CSCL, we believe that kids should be encouraged to admit when they have messed up, take action to right a wrong, and be reassured by those around them that they are loved even when in error.

Ida was new to our school in second grade. Almost immediately, she began telling her teacher that a classmate was calling her names. This continued for several days; in the meantime, other students began to go to the teacher to tell her that it was Ida who was calling her classmate names. Interactions with Ida and her classmate were fruitless as Ida continued to maintain that she was the victim. Finally, there was breakthrough. Before the first month was out, the drama teacher sensed she should share a time when she didn't tell the truth about a situation in school. Ida confessed that she felt terrible and that she had lied. The drama teacher prayed with Ida as she repented. Ida apologized not only to the one classmate, but to all her classmates. Freedom allows wrong attitudes, lies children and adults believe, and sin issues to come forth so these can be brought to light, dealt with in a healthy manner, and replaced with truth and love.

5. Protect the Culture

The staff at CSCL is very intentional to foster and protect our kingdom culture. As principal, it is my duty to recruit teachers, adjunct staff, volunteers, and other personnel who will be gatekeepers and watchmen of the unique way of learning and family atmosphere at CSCL. Once identified, I must provide training for those new to our school and arrange continual support for all who work here. I do this by holding teacher training days before the start of the school year. In addition to going over requirements, policy, and school guidelines, seasoned staff members and I introduce the kingdom concepts of freedom, honor,

This year we held "Culture and Community Days" for all the staff during the first two days of the teachers' return to CSCL. Trusted leaders and I, together with our teachers and volunteers, celebrated our unique atmosphere. We reviewed the mission statement, gave testimonies, worshipped, prayed, ate together, role played, painted, flew paper airplanes, took a personality test and compared notes, asked questions, answered questions, and commissioned the staff as fellow members in kingdom education. The result was a fully unified and cohesive body of teachers who are able to protect and promote kingdom culture.

responsibility, etc. It is our goal to free them from any constraints they have from past teaching experiences, to urge them to teach under the anointing, and to cast vision for the presence of the Lord at school.

Each teacher, member of CSCL administration, and volunteer understands that they too must protect the CSCL culture. Each is charged to get to know the students under their care, both to help the students and to prevent disruption or disunity in the school. Faculty "cover" students who make a mistake, which is not the same as to pretend that it didn't happen. Covering allows the student to recover with honor and to grow in the Lord (I Peter 4:8; Galatians 6:1). During corporate meetings, care is taken to cultivate the presence of the Lord without pressuring students (or staff) to go along with whatever the majority is doing. This is tricky—our heart wants everyone to be involved, but sometimes students are distracted by personal issues. We must honor that while keeping these students from distracting others. Students feel safe: eventually personal struggles are overcome, risks are taken, small triumphs are commended. If, however, a student continually repeats dangerous or unsafe behavior without change, he/she will be released from CSCL to safeguard the other students and preserve our culture.

Summary: The Key

The key component of education that is "kingdom" is that children encounter God. I prepare our staff to make the most of every moment to do just that. The school experience at CSCL from start to finish is crafted to allow each student to discover who Jesus is, who they are (identity), and the unique purpose that they were created to fulfill. Part of the CSCL atmosphere of freedom is that each teacher has a personal instructional style, each has a creative bent, each has a skill set specific to the subject taught, and each is permitted to set rules and procedures within the classroom. Each staff member brings a distinctive "flavor" to CSCL, while respecting and operating within the culture. And that allows all of us, teachers and students alike, to thrive.

CSCL hosts the Kingdom Educator Immersion, a two-day event, held during the school day for teachers and administrators interested in observing classes, chapels, and our culture. (For more information please contact our school office.)

CHAPTER 2

BUILDING A MINDSET TO PRODUCE KINGDOM CULTURE IN YOUR SCHOOL

by Michael Fickess

When Jesus told the parable of the wineskins, He gave us an important key as leaders—we will not be able to hold the "new wine" of what the Lord is doing unless we can remain soft, flexible, and willing to be stretched. This principle is something that has guided the staff at CSCL for a long time and it may be our most important key to success. However, this does not mean that spiritual life at our school is chaotic—for a "new wineskin" does not represent a lack of structure, but simply a different *kind* of structure. Our goal is to build a structure that is flexible enough to be an environment where the Spirit of God can move, where teachers have freedom to follow His leading, and where students are given many opportunities to grow in their gifts or be confronted with the reality and truth of who God is in our midst. There are some basic mindsets we have developed at CSCL and often re-visited throughout each school year to create the environment for this new wineskin.

Facet #1:

We are building an airplane "mid-flight."

If we are really a new wineskin, then we must fight the tendency to keep things the same from year to year. This requires prophetic creativity and imagination. In the summer before the Lord called me to serve as Bible teacher at CSCL, He gave me a recurring vision of an airplane. In the vision, the airplane was soaring higher and higher from one year to the next and it never came down. However, there was one detail of the vision that disturbed me—the airplane was still under construction and new parts were being added each year. When I saw this, I was worried that the plane would crash. But as I kept watching, I could see something deeply reassuring—the reason the airplane could not crash, despite being in mid-construction, is because the invisible hand of the Lord was keeping it aloft and lifting it higher from year to year.

As educators and leaders in the body of Christ, we want to develop a model for spiritual development that works well, so that we can create hunger for the kingdom of heaven in our students and export it around the world. This impulse to be a good steward is one reason we have developed Bible curriculum books for imparting the basic truths students need to walk with God. However, in order to be the kind of stewards God is looking for, we have to realize that the primary thing we are exporting is not a model or a curriculum, but a *mindset*.

The curriculum books might be an important part of the airplane, but there are many other critical parts that God has added over the years—things like student-led worship, "soaking" in class time, spiritual activations, or small group discussion time. God keeps our wineskins soft by continually bringing in new students and staff members from different backgrounds, resulting in an ever-shifting kaleidoscope of spiritual life on campus. However, the one thing that remains consistent is a culture of being flexible, relying on the Lord, and yielding to the new thing He is doing. These basic mindsets might seem simple at first glance, but they require vigilance in order to work on an organizational level. To be honest, there seems to be a recurring "crisis point" several times each year where we realize we need to re-visit how we are facilitating morning chapel, Bible class, special assemblies, or student life on campus. The problem is usually not that we have been doing things wrong— but that the Lord is calling us to do things *differently* because He has plans for something different in the next season. This is exactly what the children of Israel were forced to do when they followed the pillar of fire through the desert. Every time they got settled down and comfortable, the presence of God visited again and called them to pack up and go a different direction.

Mindset #2:

The people God is bringing are keys to what He is building each year.

As Rick Joyner often points out, the people that God is bringing to us at MorningStar often give a clue of what the new wineskin is meant to look like for each chapter of our ministry's history. In order to really discern what God is doing each year, we need to reflect on some concrete questions about our staff and student body development, with reflections such as:

- What is God building here?

- What kind of staff and students is He bringing?

- What makes these personnel different than what God brought us in previous seasons?

- What are the new trends we are seeing, based on who is being called here?

- What are the *consistent* aspects of who God has called our school to be from year to year, no matter who is called to come or be sent out?

- Where do I fit in the big picture?

In order to keep in step with the Spirit, it is usually important to re-visit these big questions every year, if not many times throughout the year (see Galatians 5:25). These questions also help us to maintain staff and student changes with a positive mindset. For example, when someone is called to leave, it's simply because the wineskin is changing and God wants to bring a new direction. It is dangerous and counter-productive to try to keep someone when the Lord is calling them out. Likewise, when someone with a unique gift-set comes, such as the ability to teach Mandarin Chinese or teach pottery, we look for where they fit in the larger picture of what the Lord is doing. In some cases, we also need to consider who the Lord is *not* bringing into our community. In some cases, it helps to preserve our long-term values to be more selective in choosing staff and students so that we can both navigate change more effectively and screen out anyone who would not help us to fulfill our purpose.

Mindset #3:

Blessed are the flexible: They will not snap when there is inevitable change.

As a gardener, I have recently begun building wattle fences around my garden beds—these are types of fences made from weaving branches together. I always choose green, flexible young trees to weave together because they can bend into a variety of fun and useful designs for my landscape. Occasionally, I accidentally pick a stick that is too old and brittle. As soon as I start to bend it, it breaks and I have to through it into my fire pit. Likewise, we are most useful to the Lord when we remain soft and flexible in His hands. It is only when we are unwilling to navigate and embrace the inevitable changes God will bring that we become dry, brittle, and not useful for what He is doing.

Flexibility is not the same as not having a plan. Rather, flexibility means that we are willing to lay down our plans when we are called to do so—even when they are excellent. I often tell my Bible and English students, "You can be spontaneous if you have a plan to depart from. But if you don't have a plan at all, that's chaos."

On one hand, we have a clear school schedule, our teachers submit lesson plans, and we follow a rigorous Bible program. And yet, we give our staff and students the freedom to follow the Spirit spontaneously whenever He moves. We have been known to cancel two hours of classes because students were having strong encounters with the Lord in the morning, only to resume regular classes later in the day. Likewise, teachers regularly take rabbit trails from set curriculum to follow a strong class discussion wherever it may lead, a diversion that often builds stronger critical thinking skills than a rigid teacher-dominated lesson.

The reason flexibility must be re-taught in Christian schools is because most education systems have become notoriously *inflexible*. In order to re-shape the culture, we must lead the way by giving teachers and students greater freedom. This does not mean that we will not ask for lesson plans from teachers or academic assignments from students—it means that we will allow them to pursue what the Lord is leading them to do, even when it is different than what has happened in the past. In other words, the freedom that we give to our staff and students is what empowers us to be flexible—and ultimately follow the Lord.

Mindset #4:

Develop the short-term and long-term patience of a gardener.

Gardeners have to learn both short-term and long-term patience. When I sow seeds in the spring, I have to allow enough time in the short-term for them to germinate, usually around 7-14 days. As I wait for them to germinate, my job is to make sure that the environment is ideal for germination. This might mean covering them on a cold night to protect the seeds or watering them when the weather is too dry. Likewise, it is not enough to simply teach and impart the spiritual content and academic lessons we offer. We also must maintain an environment that is ideal for learning to thrive. As an English teacher who often likes to include some college-level literary critique in my classes, this might mean using the same challenging terminology for a full two weeks until students have been exposed enough to the new vocabulary to internalize it.

As a Bible teacher in morning chapel, patience might involve letting some students pray for healing while other students simply observe what is happening. If we understand the principle of the seed properly, then some students come to us with many seeds already sown into them; they may be spiritually thriving because they have had spiritual gifts demonstrated and practiced in their lives for over a decade. In contrast, other students who are called here may be getting introduced to the things of the Spirit for the first time in their lives. Obviously, I will need to focus much more on creating the right environment and being patient with these students. However, ultimately patience calls us to trust the power of the seed itself—God often has a multi-year trajectory for student growth and the breakthroughs will often come at times and in ways that we least expect. This dynamic is further compounded by the fact that the progression of growth that God intends for each student might ultimately look different—or be on a different timeframe—than what we *want* as teachers and parents.

Recently, two young ministry leaders I know who had only been in ministry a few years began making some tragic mistakes. I became alarmed at what was happening in their ministries and I became somewhat critical about what they were doing. However, the Lord rebuked me and spoke to me in gardening language I could understand. The Father showed me a vision of two beautiful and mature fruit trees and said: "You don't cut down your fruit trees when they are only two or three years old. So, how dare you judge My fruit trees when they are only two or three years old. You need to begin to see My fruit trees as I do—after two or three decades of growth and pruning, when they are fully mature and bearing fruit."

Of course, I realized the Father was talking about how *He* saw these young ministers. He wasn't angry with the mistakes they were making because He saw the full picture of their lives, from beginning to end. Instead of being frustrated with the present, He was focused on the process and the ultimate fruit that would come from years of maturity in the future. While this revelation was initially about the Lord's perspective on ministries in the body of Christ, it has obvious application to the teenagers we teach too. How often do we get frustrated by the mistakes that teenagers make, as they navigate the challenges of life, the temptations of this world, and the pressures of the

21st century? However, we need to practice seeing every student that the Lord brings us through the Father's eyes, which means through a long-term perspective of life-time growth.

As a Bible teacher, I am always grateful for the students who take practical teachings about the things of God and begin to practice them immediately. It is satisfying to see the seeds of spiritual teaching find rich ground and germinate quickly. However, I am also aware that, in many cases, I am sowing seeds for the future. Some of the students I am teaching may not put the spiritual lessons they are learning into practice until they face a time of difficulty and heart-searching a decade from now. Others won't really discover who they are called to be until they have several more years of spiritual growth and development. I have to remind myself that what really counts is the quality of the seed and creating the right environment. In terms of stewardship, both as teachers and spiritual leaders, these are our primarily responsibilities. However, the time and place where the seed actually begins to take root and grow is up to the Lord.

Mindset #5:

Cultivate a Balance of Word and Spirit

Jesus warned the Pharisees: **"You are in error because you do not know the Scriptures or the power of God" (Matthew 22:29).** In order to have a healthy spiritual life at your school, you must have a balance of both *Word* and *Spirit*. This means we must train students in the basics of doctrine, while also providing ample opportunities for the Spirit of God to move. If we emphasize the Word alone, then we risk becoming too intellectual and analytical to be of any spiritual value. Likewise, if we only emphasize spiritual gifts, then we do not give students the deep roots of understanding they will need to sustain them later in life—which ultimately could result in them "falling away" from the faith in the future.

While our school offers curriculum books designed with this balance in mind, the real balance comes in the face-to-face encounters between staff and students that happen every day. The best way to have a balance of Word and Spirit is to recruit and train staff and students who are grounded in the Word and abide in the Spirit on a daily basis. Students are not just looking for theoretical knowledge about God, they are searching for authenticity in their walk with God. Students are looking for role models who truly "walk the walk" they are talking about. For this reason, we labor to retain a core group of staff and students who have a real and authentic walk with God to serve as role models and mentors for others who are just beginning their upward journey. The real impartation of Word and Spirit that happens at our school usually occurs in hallways and small conversations, as students get prayer from others in their time of need or process their "big questions" about God in small discipleship groups, or with a staff member they may feel safe with.

Mindset #6:

Rely on the Lord in your content development and daily execution.

A shallow version of relying on the Lord asks Him to bless *our* plans. However, it is much more effective if we rely on the Lord in order to see and implement *His* plans. Whether we are teaching science, English, math, art, or Bible, our teachers are encouraged to ask the Lord for prophetic creativity in finding new ways to teach core subjects, while also imparting the kingdom of heaven. Principal Sandy Woods refers to this as, "teaching from the third heaven." This doesn't mean that every teacher ascends to heaven when we plan lessons, but rather we are actively seeking the Lord on everything we do, just as David habitually "inquired of the Lord" before every battle.

While I have mentioned our curriculum books several times in this chapter, I chose not to use them this year because the Lord led me to focus on the essential Christian doctrines of Hebrews 6 as well as focus on inner healing and character development. Even though it would have been easier to just go with the program that He had already given me, I knew it would be more effective to obey the voice of the Lord and shift gears in response to His leading. Regardless of your location, the size of your school, or the curriculum you are using, the Lord wants to be personally involved in guiding *what* you teach and *how* you teach it. Jesus promised us that He would provide this kind of leadership for us when we need it:

"When he has brought out all his own, he goes on ahead of them, and his sheep follow him because they know his voice" (John 10:4).

Whether you are involved in leading a Christian school or homeschooling your children, the Lord has already brought you out of a broken and corrupt education system. Now, you need to trust Him to fulfill the rest of His promise—to personally speak to you and lead you on the best path forward for educating and imparting the kingdom of heaven to the next generation.

The best way to respond to this truth and cultivate this mindset is to live a lifestyle of daily consecration and invocation. When you sit down to write your lesson plans or have a staff meeting, invite the Lord to speak to you. Before you begin the day, invite the Lord to take over your classroom. Some of our teachers take time to anoint every desk before the school year begins, while others are more spontaneous and have learned to recognize when the Lord is moving in a particular class discussion. A good way to look at this concept is through the vision of Christ's words to the Laodicean church: Christ is standing at your *classroom* door knocking, and He has promised:

"If anyone hears my voice and opens the door, I will come in and eat with that person, and they with me" (Revelation 3:20).

One response to this promise of Jesus is to recognize that the Lord wants to lead and guide our plans every day and to adjust our mindset to include the willingness to hear and obey Him about daily practical things. He can give us prophetic creativity on everything from seating arrangements to writing assignments. However, in a much more direct sense, major shifts often happen through very simple and deliberate prayers, with simple words, such as, "Lord, I give You my classes today. I invite You to adjust my plans and take over." In some cases, you may even want to ask your students to invite the Lord with you and explain the value of making the Lord the center of what we do.

After you have made a habit of inviting the Lord daily into your sphere of influence in the classroom, remember that He is faithful and start looking for what He is saying and doing. Often, His leading can come in the form of a new thought or idea we didn't have before. In these cases, He will lead us to do something that will shift our habits and break us out of a mundane routine. However, the Lord also does not want to exhaust us with constant changes. For this reason, there are other times when the Lord will affirm we're already going the right direction and we just need to **"not grow wearing in doing good"** because **"at the proper time, we will reap a harvest**

if we do not give up" (see Galatians 6:9). In other words, sometimes we will be led to shift what we are *doing*, while other times we will need to shift what we are *thinking*.

Mindset #7:

Work as a team.

In I Corinthians, Paul explains that we are the "body of Christ" and we have the "mind of Christ" (see I Corinthians 2:16; 12). However, in both cases, we only have full functionality in having Christ's mind or being His body when we have every member functioning in their gift and actively contributing to the conversation. In terms of vision-setting and planning, we rely heavily on every teacher's wisdom and input. We realize that we can only get a full picture of what Christ is thinking, saying, and doing if we share our perspectives and fit them together like puzzle pieces. This is a process we follow for the larger, yearly vision for our school, but also a weekly process in other areas of school life. For example, in the Bible program, I know I am gifted at teaching about the deep things of God, but I often lack the emotional intelligence and situational awareness to discern how students are processing and internalizing what I'm teaching. For this reason, I rely on other staff members (and sometimes even mature students) to give me honest feedback and ideas to make what we are doing in Bible each week more effective. In a similar way, our elementary teachers often meet together to strategize how to solve problems and move the elementary classes higher in academics and pursuit of the Lord.

There is no substitute for having trustworthy staff members who have years of experience and wisdom. We are forced to lean on each other for feedback and help because this kind of inter-personal dependency is how God designed us to function. Even in terms of student life, we must recognize that every student contributes something very specific to their class when they are functioning in their calling and destiny. For this reason, we may intentionally call students to serve as small-group discussion leaders in chapel or Bible sessions or recruit students to lead in particular areas of their gifting or expertise.

We are accustomed to trusting that the Lord is our Provider in the area of finances. However, when you are working in a school that aspires to create the culture of heaven on earth, you also have to trust that the Lord will provide the right people— at the right time—for your staff and your student body. He always provides who we need at the right time, but it is our job as leaders to recognize gifts in staff and students, train them, and challenge them to rise and shine.

Conclusion

Principal Sandy Woods often emphasizes that our goal is to, "build the kind of school that God dreams about." In order to do this, we need a constant flow of revelation to show us what the Father is "saying and doing" each year (see John 5:19). However, getting revelation of the Father's heart for students and for Spirit-filled schools is actually the easy part. Much more difficult is the willingness to lay down our plans and remain flexible as the Lord shifts the emphasis or culture of our school from year to year. This ongoing flexibility is probably the most important lesson we have learned—and the most important attribute for other schools to adopt.

CHAPTER 3

CREATING A SAFE LEARNING ENVIRONMENT

by Erin Newbury Hogan

Creating a safe learning environment is an important part of kingdom education. When children feel comfortable and safe, they have the freedom to learn in the way their brain was created. There are three ways that I create this environment in my classroom.

The first and most important thing I do is genuinely care about my students. I acknowledge and address the academic, behavioral, and emotional challenges of my students, but these challenges do not influence my belief in their future. I believe that my students can do whatever the Lord is calling them to do. My job as a kingdom educator is to partner with parents to give the children the tools needed to overcome challenges. I also pray over my students and ask the Lord to show me how He views them.

For example, I teach fourth grade and one of my students, Beth, struggles with reading and spelling. After high school and college, she wants to be a detective. I believe she can pursue this career. I know this will require reading and writing, so I met with

Beth's parents and encouraged tutoring after school to work on specific reading goals. At school, Beth also receives small group instruction four days a week to work on strengthening her reading and spelling.

As a kingdom educator, I do not solely care about academics, but also helping the students develop a relationship with the Lord. Besides wanting to be a detective, Beth has a heart for worship. She is part of the student-led elementary worship team, which meets weekly during recess to plan worship songs and dances for elementary chapel. A few weeks ago, Beth asked if we could join in with the upper school during their morning worship. The older grades were having a time of prayer and prophetic worship. About thirty minutes after we joined in, Beth went up to the front and started to sing prophetically. I could sense the purity in her worship to the Lord. She was not singing to impress those around her, but because she loves the Lord. Kingdom caring allows me to see the potential, not the weakness, in my students.

The second thing I do is create a relationship with my students. The first week of school, I observe my class and ask questions to find out their interests, talents, and passions. There are several questions I like to include: what do you like to do outside of school? Do you play any sports? What is your favorite subject in school? Do you have any siblings? Through this type of conversation, I found out that Jack enjoyed science and had a pass to Discovery Place, a science museum in our city. He asked if the class could go. I booked the trip and chose a workshop that fit the unit we were studying. Jack was ecstatic that I listened to him.

Another way I develop relationship with my students is to allow them to be a part of my life and family. My grandmother, who lives in Michigan, makes an advent house for me that I share with the class each year. This is a tradition she started when I was born and an experience I get to share with my students. My grandmother also sends the class postcards and other crafts. I create an environment that encourages parent and grandparent involvement. I have had several grandparents, including my own, spend the day in my classroom.

I have two young children that my family members helped care for while I was at work. When my daughter was young, my mother would bring her to visit the class. Since I taught my students in both third and fourth grade, one of the students made the comment, "We got to see your daughter grow up. When you first started teaching us she was a baby and we got to see her learn to crawl, walk, talk, and now become a big sister." I show the class pictures of my children and let them interact with them. Relationship is important in a classroom setting. If students have a relationship with their teacher, they are more willing to work hard and take educational risks. For example, if a student in my class does not understand a math problem, a grammar concept, or is struggling with their class work, he or she always asks for help. I make sure that when students are working independently, I am circulating to answer questions and help those that need support. One day I was out and I had a sub. One of my students did not understand the math lesson. Sam did not know the sub and was not comfortable asking for help and was not able to do the work, so he started talking to his neighbor instead of doing the assignment. Once Sam became comfortable with the sub, he asked for help and started working.

The third thing I do is modify instruction to meet the academic and emotional needs of the class. As a teacher at a small school, I quickly learn the needs of the class. One year, my class had varying reading needs. CSCL decided to offer small group instruction to my class. CSCL trains teachers and parent volunteers in multisensory phonics, based on the Orton Gillingham approach. This allows all kindergarten through third grade students to receive one hour of small group reading instruction per day. The group sizes range from two students up to five. Small group instruction is not something typically offered in fourth grade. However, since the students in my class needed more reading support, the reading specialist was able to organize enough volunteers to offer my class small group instruction. The students were able to work on the skills they needed to be successful.

There are more simple ways to modify instruction, such as giving students extended time on a test, or reading a test aloud. If students know their teacher's goal is to help them be successful, it eliminates a lot of anxiety. Modifying instruction is a balancing act. As a teacher, my goal is to challenge students, but not drive them to perform a task they are not ready for. For example, I do not force students to read aloud in front of the class. The other day, Jack, a struggling reader, volunteered to read during our novel study. This year the class read *Tales of a Fourth Grade Nothing* by Judy Bloom. We read the novel together. Each student is given the opportunity to read a page in the novel. The other students follow along with the reader in their own book. If Sam had not felt safe, he would not have had the courage to read in front of his class.

My current class has many talents and strengths, but some struggle with academics. Because the class is a safe learning environment, every single student works hard and has a positive self-image. This was not the case at another school I worked at prior to teaching at CSCL. Many of those that struggled had a poor self-image. As a Kingdom Educator, I have the opportunity to provide students with a safe learning environment where they can pursue the Lord, rather than forcing them to learn the way society expects.

CHAPTER 4

TRANSMITTING KINGDOM CULTURE

by Trace White

Kingdom culture is *caught* as much as it is taught. Teaching alone would be insufficient to pass it on to the next generation. People have to feel it, experience it, and see it in living color so that they can embrace it, own it, and choose to live it.

One of the most effective ways I have seen kingdom culture perpetuated is through mentoring relationships. Mentoring is the most common word we use today for discipleship. Jesus mentored His followers by modeling, teaching, empowering, and correcting while always relating to His disciples in love with healthy boundaries. These processes are integral to transmitting kingdom culture.

Modeling

Beyond giving instruction in the subject matter of our disciplines, we are always teaching by modeling. Students understand what the nature of the kingdom of God looks like by how we relate to them. We incubate the kingdom culture in them by treating them with respect and significance, looking to see the real person, the authentic self, the original design, and speaking to them as individuals. I often think about how Jesus treated people and seek His guidance in challenging situations so that I will respond in concert with what the Father is doing. That is how He treated the ones who were constantly trying to trap Him. Though they functioned as His enemies, He always treated them with respect and honor.

One of the most effective times to model the culture of the kingdom is during times of failure. How we treat people when they are not exhibiting their best selves tells a lot about who we are. One of my students, Jack (not his real name), was standing nervously by my desk. He'd been talking incessantly during class and had been using his cell phone even after I had requested that he put it away. I had collected it; now he wanted it back. What I wanted was a deeper commitment from him to be who he really was. His behavior had not portrayed his true self. He came to apologize and get the phone. I wanted to talk about why he had been acting in a dishonoring way, when that wasn't who he really was. I don't know what he expected, but I could tell by his posture that he was in defensive mode and ready to do battle. My approach was to affirm the positive that I saw in him, express acceptance of him as a highly esteemed person, and see if we could come to an agreement that he would live by his own values while he was in my class and beyond. Not only did Jack agree to do so, he opened up and told me about what was going on in his family life and how distraught he was over the tensions in the home. The situation totally changed between us. By modeling the kingdom way of relating, an opportunity was created for real connection and breakthrough.

Practical thoughts:

- Lead by example
  - Do not require anything of students that you do not do yourself.

- Speak in the manner and tone that you want to be spoken to.

- Hold yourself accountable to the same standards that you set for others.

- Take off the "professional" appearance and have fun!

- Confess if you are wrong and apologize if necessary.

• Seek to understand who the student really is

- What is their story? Who are they?

- How does life look for them outside of your classroom?

- What are they going through?

- Ask God to show you who they really are in Him.

- Notice who their friends are. What does that tell you about them?

• Build genuine connection with the student

- Have conversation with them about what is important to them.

- Take opportunities to encourage when possible, but do not flatter.

- Look students in the eye. See them.

- Play games in class whenever possible.

- Work on projects together.

Teaching

Following the lead of the Holy Spirit is crucial for teaching. He is the Lead Tutor, and He has a plan. One of my memorable God moments was with a class of 7th graders. It was a day when I had laryngitis, so I had to write instructions on the whiteboard. The class became unusually quiet in order to receive and follow the instructions. One of the students remarked on how the whole class had become collectively more attentive and focused, due to everyone having to listen so closely to my hoarse, whispered instructions. This created a student-led discussion about self-management, self-control, and maturity—they realized they were having to change their behavior to hear me more clearly, and they saw a parallel to growing in maturity in hearing the voice of the Holy Spirit. I gave space during the class time for this, as I understood it to be a divine appointment. I sensed that the Holy Spirit had an agenda that I needed to follow. One of the ongoing challenges in kingdom education is being able to listen to the Holy Spirit and follow His lead even when it may seem completely foreign to conventional thinking and practice. The more attuned we are, the more breakthroughs we experience. In this particular instance, life lessons were being learned, *both* for me and for the students. This became a new point of reference for the class that I could return to at various times during the rest of the semester. It also created an opportunity for me to teach on human motivations and how we make choices.

Practical thoughts:

- Seek the Holy Spirit—He is the real Teacher
    - Ask the Holy Spirit for insights while you are doing your lesson planning.
    - Carry a serendipity notepad (or smartphone) to write down spontaneous revelations.
    - Observe what He is doing while class is going on.
    - Be open for a change of plans!

- Look for the genius in each student—it is there
  - Each student is created in the image of the Almighty.
  - Help them see their own genius.
  - Be a goldminer—search for what is going well and point it out.
  - Speak words of life over them when you are with them.
  - Speak words of life over them when you are not with them.
  - See them through Jesus' eyes.

- Give clear guidelines
  - Produce the guidelines in printed form.
  - Refer to the guidelines often to reinforce expectations.
  - Have students repeat the guidelines—it helps to deepen the impression

i.e., "We are listening when someone else is talking." "Doing my best is my commitment to excellence."

- Utilize multi-sensory engagement
  - Engage the whole brain.
  - Infuse critical thinking whenever possible.
  - Use problem solving as a method for learning.

- Be conscious of contemporary attention spans
  - Kids today work well in intermittent periods of time.
  - Allow for stop-and-go work times.
  - Rotate classwork that involves different sets of skills.

- Give meaningful, age-appropriate projects that work both individually and in teams

- In-class projects give teachers the chance to observe students as they work.
- Connect projects to real life lessons.
- Allow students to present their project to others.
- Praise whatever is praiseworthy.

• Show relevance between the biblical knowledge and your class content

- The Bible is the foundational textbook for all subject matter.
- How does Jesus and His teachings relate to what you are teaching?
- What stories in Scripture demonstrate a point you are trying to make?
- What parallels do you see between situations today and those in the Bible?

• Play games

- Kids love to play, and games make information easier to retain.
- Kids trust adults that can "let down their hair" and play with them.
- Challenge students to create their own games as a project.
- Use improv, drama, and icebreakers to open hearts and minds.

• Role reversal—let the kids teach wherever they can

- If they can teach it, then they probably know it.
- Coach students prior to role-reversal exercises.
- Affirm, affirm, affirm!

- It is important for the students to also see us as real people. Role reversal exercises help with this.
- Have reflection times after role reversals. Talk about how it was for them, and draw out the lessons for sensitivity training.

Empowering

Empowerment is one of the major goals of kingdom education. It is about creating an environment, practice, and process to foster the release of the authentic self of every individual. Each of us has been created by the Father from the foundation of the world for the purposes of His pleasure. There is a resident potential within every student that is waiting to be released. There is genius, brilliance, and aptitude in each student. We are mining for that treasure. Many of them are not aware of their own prowess.

The main purpose of kingdom education is to create alignment in the lives of students with the great commandment and the great commission. This means that it will be a transformational educational experience which permeates every facet of school life, so the students will learn how to have relationship with God and others, discover who they are, develop their unique giftings, and be prepared for release into their destiny for kingdom advancement.

There are two primary ways that we are empowered. In the natural, it functions by choice, through opportunities that we create or that are extended to us by others. The other way we are empowered is supernaturally by the power and will of God. We need both. By entrusting students with their own power of choice (developmentally appropriate), we are giving them the tools for learning to live as *"response-able"* individuals. By connecting them with the supernatural life, we are releasing them to their destinies as men and women of God.

Ownership is another essential element of an empowered life. It is fundamental to kingdom culture and must find its place within kingdom schools. Ownership means that the students take responsibility for their speech, behavior, and way of being as they are able (just like the situation with Jack. He was being held to a higher level of accountability in accordance with who he is in Christ). We are partnered with the Holy Spirit in raising free sons and daughters. This is our inheritance in the kingdom of God.

We had a visitor come to our class one day. She wanted to observe how the school operated. One of the ways that we empower students is to release them to give prophetic words. We believe that the Holy Spirit will manifest Himself through them. When the class was coming to a close, I asked if the students could pray for our visitor. She consented, and they surrounded her as they began to pray. Soon, different students were getting prophetic words for her and speaking into her life! She told me later that they had been so accurate and encouraging. The Lord used these teenagers to confirm things in her life that she had been seeking Him about that only He would know. The students were responsible for their words and took ownership of the experience by releasing prophetic words as an extension of who they are in Him.

Ownership is a higher level of commitment, which produces a significantly different level of engagement. While compliance may produce order, ownership almost guarantees transformational activity, both in the students' lives and for those within their sphere of influence. Free people are more creative, more innovative, exercise more critical thinking, and solve more problems. It is a natural effect of the paradigms associated with empowerment.

Practical thoughts:

- Integrate the supernatural as a natural part of everyday experience
  - Ask God to show up.
  - Pray with students and have them pray for each other.
  - Share things from your own experience (successes and failures).
  - Encourage students to take appropriate risks.
  - Be attentive to what the Holy Spirit is doing in your midst (especially through students—have learned some of my best lessons like this).
- Set the expectation for them to give their best
  - Identity exercises are very helpful for self-discovery and empowerment.
  - Assess each student's confidence level.
  - Build confidence where necessary.
- Create opportunities for experimentation
  - Let them "pull their own wagon" as soon as they are ready.
  - Be more permission-giving than permission-withholding.
  - Lead them to lean on God.
- Seek for students to have ownership in their educational experience
  - Entrust them with real power whenever possible—

the more students can lead themselves, the less we need to manage.

- Solicit "buy-in" at every level of the school experience.
- Formulate some kind of covenant or agreement for students to sign.

- Set them up for success
  - Create situations so students can be successful if they invest the effort.
  - Create boundaries/expectations around the experiment.
  - Help students to identify the desired outcome.
  - Create situations where students are stretched to experience success.

- Let students solve their own problems
  - Help the student to see their responsibility in the situation.
  - Ask them what they need to do to fix it.
  - Use role reversal as a strategy ("what would you want done?").
  - Seek mediation only where necessary.

- Hold students accountable to their commitments
  - Have students communicate their commitment verbally or in writing.
  - Have them keep their word.
  - "Reset the clock" if needed. Do they need to recommit to something?

- Allow students to experience the results of their choices for better or worse
  - Reward positive choices.

- Allow the consequence for negative choices.
- Show grace while enforcing the consequences.
- Choose truth over pseudo-peace "peace."

Correcting

Correction is a natural phase in the process of learning. It is essential in the transmission of kingdom culture. Once goals have been set and attempts have been made to realize those goals, an objective assessment can be made and instruction given to correct any shortcomings. Students should *expect* to be held accountable and learn how accountability works so that they can implement it in their own relationships. Adjustments can only be made after the assessment and correction phase. Without this, mastery cannot be attained.

This, however, means dealing with failure at some level. Students should understand that failure is a part of the learning cycle so they can face it without shame or judgment. Taking the shame and judgment out of the equation is paramount. Gracious responsibility is at the core of kingdom culture. It liberates us to become masters rather than merely practitioners.

Me: *Janice, could we talk for a minute or so?*

Janice: *Sure. Am I in trouble?*

Me: *I just want to speak to you about what you had promised to do.*

Janice: *Oh, yes. I have been meaning to talk to you about that.*

Me: *I'm all ears.*

Janice: *I haven't done it yet. I don't have a good reason why. I apologize.*

Me: *Can I expect that you will still follow through?*
Janice: *Yes, and I will let you know as soon as it is done.*
Me: *Thanks so much.*

Once correction is embraced as a part of the learning process and shame has been removed, confession can surface like a breath of fresh air. In my classes, we use a phrase, "tell on yourself." This encourages the valuable method of self-correction. It functions on the assumption that we will hold ourselves accountable for our words and actions.

As humans, we tend to learn more from our failures than our successes. This is an organic reality in life. Using the example of learning how to walk, toddlers master the art of walking through trial and error. The natural consequence of falling when the child fails is a reminder of how to do it differently when they make their next attempt. Because parents do not pass shame or negative judgment on the activity, the child continues to try, no matter how many times they fail, and eventually they learn to walk. If this reality, which reflects God's interaction with us, can be translated into the classroom and school culture, failure can always be turned into a learning experience which empowers the student.

Practical thoughts:

- Plan one-on-one assessment/correction times in private
  - Schedule meetings outside of class time for the sake of privacy.
  - Meet on their "turf" or in a neutral place, if possible.
  - Speak with parents only after speaking with the student.

- Revert to covenants, agreements, or written outlines as a means of accountability.

- Seek to make aware and alert—knowing how to evaluate is as important as the goal setting

  - Use the Socratic method. Ask lots of penetrating questions.

  - Do not readily give answers. Let students figure out what they can.

  - Encourage proactivity.

- Have students self-assess regularly

  - The more we judge ourselves, the less others need to.

  - Use 360° evaluations to take the shame out of assessments.

  - Include reflections exercises periodically.

  - Identify how the failure happened.

- Entertain discussions which are solution-oriented

  - Engage other students when appropriate.

  - Work and evaluate in teams.

  - Explore "win/win" options.

Conclusion

Educating impressionable young people is a weighty undertaking. It requires copious amounts of love, grace, understanding, forbearance, and discipline. This is not an activity for the faint of heart. It is a task that we are unable to accomplish without the potency of the Holy Spirit. We are partnering with the Lord in rearing up a company of royals. We will be taking possession of the kingdoms of this world together. They are called to scale the dizzying heights of every elevated entity which defines culture in our world and bring redemption to it (i.e. the 7 Mountain Mandate).

In order for this to happen, our "ceiling must become their floor." We have the amazing privilege and responsibility of helping to prepare the "Joshua generation" to usher in God's eternal kingdom. This makes kingdom education a thoroughly holistic work. It is imperative that we are consistently "on our game." Kingdom education requires a mentoring commitment which mirrors that of Jesus with His disciples. And for this substantial investment, we shall reap incomprehensible rewards in this life and the one to come.

CHAPTER 5

WHAT IS SCHOOL?

by Donna Reynolds

What should school be like in kingdom education? This is a question I have been asking myself for many years. I came to CSCL three years ago, having taught in various educational settings as an elementary English and History teacher. I have been learning ever since.

One night, I had a dream that led me to some answers about what kingdom education really looks like. Some people dream every night. I am not one of them. Usually I dream when God has something significant He wants to say to me. In my dream, I was in a school bus that was turning a corner and going uphill. I looked out the window to my right and saw many school buses passing me. They were larger buses, hooked together like piggyback tractor-trailers, traveling in a downward direction. That was all that happened in the dream. I woke up puzzled, wondering what the dream meant. The next few hours would shed light on this dream.

That same day, I came to school in time to teach my 11:00am 5th grade writing class. As I walked down the hallway to my classroom, I heard worship coming from the main meeting room, where all the students usually gather for chapel first thing in the morning. Chapel is usually over at 8:30am, but when I rounded the corner, I saw all of the 6th-12th grade students still worshiping the Lord. Many were sitting on the floor, in a large group, led by student musicians. The closer I got, the more I felt the glory of the Holy Spirit resting on these youths. Without hesitation, I hurried to the gym to pick up my 5th grade class. We joined the worship instead of going to writing class. Soon, an invitation was given to those that needed a miracle in their life to come forward for prayer. Many lined up for prayer with students and teachers gathering around them. I asked one of my students if she would like to pray for the sick with me. As we were praying, I heard the still small voice of the Lord whisper, "This is school."

After the prayer time, I felt the release to return to our classroom for our scheduled spelling test. I noticed I was still feeling the weighty presence of the Lord, and it was difficult for me to walk and even stand in front of the class. As a class, we talked about the recent experience. My students confirmed they were feeling the same presence even in our classroom. We decided to take the test and then return to the main room. It was a test I will never forget. All our words had an (– ly) suffix. Our first word was "totally." I said, "Lord, Your presence is totally awesome!" The Lord gave me a sentence to describe His kingdom for all twenty spelling words. Eager students with smiles on their faces returned to the main room to receive more from the great teacher, the Holy Spirit.

I did have an hour's worth of lesson plans for my writing class. I made the choice to set my agenda aside. In our school, we post our plans for parents and administrators to review. However, we have a principal that allows us to include the Holy Spirit in our plans. With that in mind, I am always listening to hear that still small voice that may cause me to change my plans. In Proverbs 16:9, the Lord tells us, **"in his heart a man plans his course, but the Lord determines his steps."** This is the process I follow for each class I teach.

My thoughts go back to the dream I had that night before. Could it be that the school bus represented kingdom education? I was traveling on this bus, going in an upward direction. I saw many buses much larger than mine going in the opposite direction. Can this bus really make a difference in the lives of these children by taking them into the realm of God's kingdom? I truly believe that the answer is yes. This is school!

Jesus must have first place in all that we do. In every class I teach, we give Him at least five minutes of "soaking" time. My students all know the procedure. After I greet them at the door, they gather their notebooks and supplies. I turn off the main lights and turn on smaller and dimmer lights. We spend time with Jesus, quietly listening to worship music. Some students like to draw, while others like to rest their heads on their desk. I also take this time to soak and wait on the Lord. This time is well spent. We receive words, pictures, and an overwhelming peace to begin our learning journey. I often end this time with a simple prayer: "Lord, give us eyes to see, ears to hear, and hearts to receive." We often share what the Lord has shown us or pray for a healing need. Headaches leave, stomachaches leave, and peace comes to anxious hearts. Once these needs are met, we can be free to enjoy learning.

Before I began this soaking time with my students, I saw the need for students to focus and receive peace before I presented the lesson. They would enter my room engaged with each other, active and chattering amongst themselves. This quiet time of soaking gave them focus and much more. Here are some comments written by students when asked the question "What does soaking mean to you?"

"When we soak, it makes me happy and I also feel the Holy Spirit in the room."

"Soaking means to me that I can spend time with the Lord, and He always gives me comfort and I feel safe when I'm with my class and with the Lord."

"For me, it means that before you do worldly work, you need to spend time with Jesus and hear from Him."

"Soaking time is so peaceful. For me, it gives me a chance to put everything behind me and focus on the Lord."

"Soaking calms me down for the rest of school and gives me time to talk with the Lord during school."

Elementary students feel peace, safety, comfort, and they hear from their heavenly Father during our soaking times. With anticipation, they look forward to this time and do not want to skip it, even if we are pressed for time. These are golden nuggets in the kingdom of heaven. I am amazed at the prophetic experiences my students have in this short amount of time. For example, two girls recounted having visions, but didn't know what they meant. Another student eagerly raised her hand to comment, "I know what each vision means." With great detail, she explained each vision and the interpretation. Later that day, I spoke with her classroom teacher, and she confirmed her revelatory gift.

Another student recounted a prophetic experience she had during soaking time in my history class: "I closed my eyes and I asked God if I could go to heaven. He flew me up to heaven but I was still in my seat. I felt a cool breeze around my head. I was flying over people there. Everyone was worshiping God. They were having a party worshipping. They were having fun worshiping God! They were jumping up and down, raising their hands. The people were also dressed up in things that represented what they love to do but couldn't do on earth. I saw a cowboy, a racecar driver, a ballerina, and many other people. It seemed like I was there for two hours!"

Another classmate raised her hand to comment, "I believe I have a word for you. It is Matthew 7:7." When asked, she didn't know what this verse meant, so we looked it up. In amazement, I read, **"Ask, and it will be given to you; seek, and you will find; knock and it will be opened to you."** With her childlike faith, she asked and God showed her heaven! I was undone, to say the least. This was my last class of the day, and I didn't want to leave my room.

I remember one day when the same primary class entered my room in complete disarray. Several students were crying, and others were trying to explain what happened. It was evident that negative words had been spoken and the result was hurt feelings and dissension. These situations can happen in a school environment, especially with our youngest students. I briefly discussed the power of our words and encouraged each of them to give the situation to Jesus. We started our soaking time and I watched while some cried with their hands cupped toward heaven. And He brought healing to their hearts. When the song ended, I asked them what they experienced. "Peace" was the unanimous response. The King had come and brought peace to our classroom. All was well and our history lesson went very well that day.

At times, more than I can recall, God has used my students to give me words of encouragement. One day, a quiet student walked up to me after our soaking time and handed me a piece of notebook paper. On it was written, "I heard God say, 'don't turn back' and I saw an eagle flapping his wings and soaring across the sky." A picture was drawn with a flying eagle and a speech bubble with the words, "Don't turn back."

Mentoring our students and giving them opportunities to grow in their gifts and callings is an important part of kingdom education. I chuckle when I remember the day we had an outside visitor, a teacher, observing our classroom. This 5th grade class loves their soaking time and always openly shares what they receive with the class. However, this time, everyone froze when I asked them to share, apparently nervous about the guest in the room. A student raised her hand and said, "What did you see and hear?" I responded, "I saw a large rock in the ocean. I was on the rock and the waves were splashing around it. I heard the words, I am your rock!" When the students noticed my willingness to share, the dam of fear was broken. They began to share their experiences. This special time with Jesus always brings us together and prepares us for the entire class.

This is school in kingdom education. We make time for the King to come and we worship Him. As teachers, we equip our students academically and provide opportunities for them to encounter their Creator. There is no greater atmosphere for learning and creativity, than to honor the Creator and His presence.

SECTION II

TESTIMONIES

CHAPTER 6

A PARENT'S PERSPECTIVE

by Charlotte Jordaan

As a parent and volunteer, I have spent many hours at CSCL over the past four years. I am there daily, and I believe that this enabled me to gain a better understanding of the day-to-day operations and activities. One of the main things I have learned is that you cannot fit CSCL into the molds of other schools. The simplest explanation is that CSCL is certainly not your average school. An average school is very tame and controlled, but there is also little life in it. CSCL, on the other hand, is more wild and untamed. I think of it sometimes like a jungle, but that means it is full of life and so much potential for discovery and growth.

As a parent, I have learned to accept the wild side of CSCL and appreciate when things get a little untamed. If you are expecting the same-old school life, I want to share my experience to help you navigate the freedom in this school. This is my perspective on freedom at CSCL.

When the Jungle Gets Loud

School can get a little loud at times, as I have noticed when I walk through the halls. A typical school is much more quiet, and I made the mistake of thinking that the quiet schools meant that the students were attentive. I have discovered that the more engaged the students are, the louder they can be—but it is not chaos or just noise, the students are permitted and even encouraged to raise their voices. The teachers have not lost control of the students. They are allowing the children to be children while they are learning, and it is an incredible sound to hear.

I walked down the passageways once and suddenly heard a whole classroom of 2nd graders roar out like they were beasts or wild animals. I wondered if the teacher was truly in control or perhaps had gotten tied up by out-of-control children. But when I looked into the classroom, the teacher was roaring right along with them—she was leading the students in a Holy Spirit inspired roar, like a lion, to really help them experience the act of faith in Scripture when God commanded the armies to yell and let Him fight on their behalf. The students were engaged in this study, and this little exercise helped them to be kids and stay engaged with what the teacher was saying—who knows what might happen next!

I have also seen students coloring away on sheets of paper, and it might seem like they are just scribbling or taking a break from learning, but I found out the teacher had asked the students to ask the Holy Spirit to show them a picture for someone and then draw it. They might not have known they were getting prophetic words, but that was exactly what they were doing. One student had drawn a picture for me, and it was just an amazing confirmation of what God had been saying to me. She handed me a crayon drawing of a rainbow and said that God told her it was for me, and that very week God had been telling me to remember His promises for me. I could not believe that the little students were being taught to hear from God so clearly. I love the freedom the students have to be wild and creative. While they are learning the basics of reading and writing, they are also learning the foundations of hearing from God in a way that fits in with their level of experience.

Self-Control vs. False Control

The wildness and freedom that is clear in every aspect of CSCL also shows up in the way they deal with "problem students" or difficult situations. In a normal school, a teacher would just automatically punish students who misbehave and that is the end of it—it may seem orderly, but what is being learned? I was a teacher's aide in a middle school classroom once when two boys started calling each other names. They had apparently had a disagreement during lunch and their argument had carried into the classroom. In most schools, each student would be punished and then a note would be sent home to their parents, perhaps the school would have set up a "no talking during lunch" policy to stop this from happening. But what I witnessed was so much better than adding rules and regulations—the teacher began teaching them.

She was not militant about rules and she did not set up restrictions to create a false sense of control in the classroom. Instead, she gave the class a reading assignment and brought the two boys to her desk. She engaged them in a discussion, asking them what had happened and why they were calling each other names. She asked engaging questions like "do you think this was right to say this about him?" and "how did your disagreement turn into name calling?" and "is this what you want to be known for?" Instead of setting up a false sense of control for them, she started teaching them about self-control and how to govern themselves and learn how to develop a third-party perspective. They thought about how their disagreement affected each other, the classroom, and their friendship, and they had to consider when they crossed the line of having a heated discussion into a verbal fight.

This mini-lesson did not take much time, but it did put the students into a situation where they had to express their feelings and communicate with each other while they were still disagreeing with each other. This freedom to express their emotions and their frustrations is so important, especially since they are learning at a young age how to navigate difficult situations without being told what to do or not do. They were learning the basic mechanisms that will help them have true discipline and self-control as they grow up. This freedom in the classroom is not anything I have seen anywhere else. As a parent, I appreciate knowing that my kids are learning conflict resolution and self-control as part of their school studies.

Holy Spirit Wisdom in Class

I have grown to appreciate the CSCL teachers who have the inspiration of the Holy Spirit to know when to bring order and when to have flexibility. I think of other schools and it must be so difficult to teach without the Holy Spirit—if we are just there to focus on work and tasks, we may get through the lessons but nothing else is covered. The Holy Spirit will bring wisdom on how to get through the lessons and also let the students be themselves. I was assisting in one elementary school class, and one of the little girls had such trouble just sitting still, especially if they were covering a subject she liked. She would just stand up and twirl or sing a little happy song—I thought the teacher might tell her to stop or put her name on the board for discipline, but instead the teacher understood that the student was not being rebellious. They had talked about when to sit still and the teacher permitted her to twirl once a day, and what a great compromise—the student got to express her joy and the teacher knew how to perceive it as creativity instead of misbehavior.

I have a few experiences with asking the Holy Spirit for real wisdom in classes that I helped teach, and it really makes a difference to have an inspired answer or plan. I was in a middle school classroom that got into a heated political discussion after the 2016 elections. One student was pro-Trump and the other was pro-Clinton. In other schools, the discussion would have either been shut down completely or the teacher might have told the students what to think. Instead, the teacher felt like there was an opportunity to demonstrate a biblical principle of praying for our leaders, whether we agree with them or not. He led the whole class in a prayer time for President Trump, asking for God's wisdom and protection for him. Then he led the whole class in a time of prayer for Hillary Clinton, thanking God for her giftings and the passion she has in her leadership. Both students were relieved that they were not shut down, and it was encouraging to hear both of them pray for the leader they did not support politically.

From my own personal teaching experience, I taught a small elective class of middle schoolers, and it was hard to maintain that level of freedom that is part of CSCL culture. I had witnessed it as a parent, but when I was put in the teacher role, I had to remember that I needed to rely on the Holy Spirit to help me through difficult situations. I had one student who got frustrated with the project because she was not interested in the topics. I kept telling her to stay focused and on the topic of the projects when she was in class—she felt like she was not able to be herself and she shut down, not participating in discussions. I asked the Holy Spirit for help in getting her engaged, and I felt I should find a common interest with this student. After a few attempts at conversations, I discovered we both loved scuba diving and had both wanted to go swimming with dolphins one day. I was able to get the conversation started with her, and after that, she started engaging in classroom discussions. Even after that class was completed, she still finds me to talk about how her pursuit of scuba diving is going and when she hopes to swim with dolphins. I appreciated the help of the Holy Spirit to bring this student back into the conversation and really help us build relationship.

Building Trust

As a parent, it is hard sometimes to not be worried about how your kids will be treated in a school. I have several kids of different ages, each with their own gifting and strengths and weaknesses. I do sometimes worry that their weakest areas of school will hold them back somehow, or I wonder how the teachers work with them to help them overcome their weaknesses. In other schools, my kids have either experienced firsthand or seen other students get singled out or labeled a "problem child" if they struggle with a specific subject.

At CSCL, though, I have noticed that teachers are careful not to label students or put them in a box. I had one teacher share with me that her most difficult student had trouble coping in class and concentrating in a classroom environment. She had prayed for this student and felt like God was drawing her closer to that child to build a relationship and help him. A few days later, I was in the hallway and I saw the student she was speaking about. I asked him how his classes were going and he said he felt like he was getting better and he liked his teacher. It was exciting to hear that even though he was a struggling student, it did not stop him from having a good working relationship with the teacher. I asked him what he liked about his teacher and he said, "I trust her." As any parent knows, this is a huge thing for a student to say!

I love sending my children to a school where the teachers really do want to help the students to learn and also grow as individuals. I know that even if my child is struggling in a certain subject that the teachers will not make them feel less important. Building trust is difficult even under the best of circumstances, and I appreciate that the teachers seek the Lord on how to get students to build relationships with them, each other, and the Lord.

Closing Thoughts

CSCL is founded on the concept of freedom. As a parent, I have learned to trust that "freedom" does not mean "chaos." Though it will get a little wild sometimes, I have grown to understand that the untamed freedom that is part of CSCL is the kind of freedom where students can be themselves, learn how to grow in self-control, and really build lasting relationships. It's a wild place, but I want my children to reach their highest potential and that comes through letting them learn how to live with freedom and be themselves.

Section II: Testimonies

CHAPTER 7

FIRE TUNNEL

by Kari Barr

I have been blessed to be a teacher at CSCL for three wonderful years. I went to a Christian school for most of my education, and I have taught the last twenty years in Christian education. I come from a very conservative background with not much knowledge on the prophetic. I struggled at first adapting to the culture at CSCL, but it has changed my life. I would like to use a yearly activation at our school to share my testimony.

At CSCL, we begin each year with what is called a "fire tunnel." We line up our staff and students into two lines, facing each other to form a "tunnel." We send each person through, and they receive prayer, prophetic words, and encouragement for the upcoming year. It is an intense time, focused on blessing and impartation that helps prepare us for the coming year. As I discovered later, there is an extreme manifestation of the Holy Spirit.

The first year I experienced the fire tunnel, I was scared to death. In my church experience, I have never seen the manifestation of the Holy Spirit in a person. I watched as a fellow teacher was overcome with emotion and fell to the floor with laughter and tears. I did not understand. I found several ways to avoid the tunnel and just observed from a distance.

The next year, I went through the fire tunnel and I felt such a powerful presence of God that I started weeping without realizing it. I was embarrassed from crying, but felt an awesome sense of relief and joy. It seemed to unlock some areas in my life where fear had taken control. I also recognized a spirit of legalism which the grace of Jesus began to change.

Since that time, I have been overwhelmed with a new sense of freedom. I was also drawn to the CSCL staff and the Lord in a way I had never experienced before. This year as I approached the fire tunnel, I felt some anxiety because there is always an element of the unknown, but I went through it. Once again, I was encouraged and blessed. By the time I got towards the end, I was renewed and refreshed by the Holy Spirit and ready more than ever to begin a new school year.

CSCL is similar to a fire tunnel. The Holy Spirit draws the students to our school and allows us to encourage and love on them. The freedom in our school can help free the students from fear or the lies of the deceiver that break down their true identity in Christ. Receiving a new identity in Christ by itself may be scary and unfamiliar, but when the students go through this together, it builds unity between them and the Lord that helps transform them into strong spiritual leaders. They discover who they are in Christ, learn their strengths and weaknesses, then emerge with a kingdom view, ready to take on whatever plan the Lord has for them.

CLASSROOM AND SCHOOL CULTURE PRACTICES

CHAPTER 8

CHAPEL: THE FOUNDATION OF KINGDOM EDUCATION

by Sheila Lester

There was a time when it seemed that every guest or perspective parent in our building would ask, "What curriculum do you use?" When they realized there was something different at Comenius School for Creative Leadership, they assumed it must be the curriculum we were following. In more recent years, the most frequently asked question is in response to our describing ourselves as a "kingdom" school. As such, we make a distinction between our approach to education as opposed to the typical paradigm of a Christian school. So, you may ask: "What is kingdom education?" That is a very good question and one that we have been pursuing in our approach to teaching and learning. Just as Comenius had reformed education in the 1600s and beyond, we believe kingdom education can bring change to the way we teach our children for generations to come. I believe Comenius was not only the father of modern education, but was, in fact, the first kingdom educator.

Where did Comenius get his inspiration for educational change? What was his vision for what it should look like? The answer is very simple. His inspiration was Scripture, and Jesus

Himself was the vision. Although Jesus taught on many topics (we may think of these as content areas), His primary focus was a call to repent, to follow Him, and a call to the reality of the kingdom of God. Throughout Scripture, He taught that the kingdom He spoke of was not heaven, but rather the reality of His rule and reign of the unseen kingdom of God. It becomes clear that His desire was that every believer know that they are citizens of His kingdom, with the full benefits of that citizenship. As a kingdom school, we have determined that Jesus' invitation to repent, to follow Him, and to know the reality of the kingdom on earth is the foundation of all that we do at CSCL. To undertake this three-fold task, we must create an atmosphere for our students to encounter Him and to repent to ensure that they are continuing to encounter Him on an ongoing basis, so they may grow in their knowledge of Him and in who He created them to be. This is what will facilitate their transformation to learn how to live in His kingdom. It is these goals that are explicit in all that we do; and it begins each day with chapel. Chapel is pervasive in all that we do. It is impossible to compartmentalize the learning and experiences that take place in chapel and continue to be a kingdom school. Like Comenius, our vision is bigger than impacting one school and a small cohort of students. Kingdom education is educational reform—it is a revolution of teaching and learning. It has the potential to raise up high-impact lovers of God who are simultaneously the bride of Christ and the army of God.

Kingdom education is both education reform and cultural reformation. Those of you familiar with the 7 Mountain Mandate (Bill Bright; Lance Wallnau; etc.) will understand when I say that we see kingdom education as being at the top of the education mountain. We have learned from these gentlemen and others that whatever ideology or practices sit at the top of each of the seven spheres of influence (7 mountains) will have the greatest impact in that sphere and, as a result, in the culture. In order to have the greatest impact, whether in your school or around the world, we must learn how to climb to the top of that mountain.

It is not enough that we as educators learn how to make this climb, but our goal is to take the students in our charge up that mountain with us. This does not mean that we assume that all our students will choose the career path of education. Instead, it means only that every student that comes to CSCL joins us in this journey. As such, they can have an educational experience different than most other students are offered. We are all familiar with Proverbs 22:6, **"Train up a child in the way he should go: and when he is old, he will not depart from it."** God has charged us with "training" these young people with how to live and be productive in what was once a foreign culture. Of course, this training begins with their parents, but it is continued in the educational setting at Comenius School that starts with chapel.

Prophetically speaking, think of chapel as the base camp at the bottom of the mountain you are preparing to climb. It is here that preparations are made that you get to know and develop trust and community with your team, and you train how to respond in different conditions. Ultimately, you learn how to live in an environment and culture which previously was foreign to you. Much like the preparation which takes place in the base camp, chapel is where we set the stage and begin to train our students, ensuring that they have opportunity to come to know the King and are learning how to live in His kingdom.

To make the notion of training to live in the kingdom more relatable, I'd like to share from my personal experience. I visited the U.K. for the first time about twenty-five years ago. Although it was an international trip, I fully expected it to be very much like being in the U.S. Because we spoke the same language and had shared history, I naively expected the only significant cultural differences to be the English accent and driving on the other side of the road. I could not have been more mistaken. More than once, I unwittingly insulted an English person by asking them to repeat themselves multiple times because I couldn't understand their "English."

On subsequent travels to places as diverse as Acapulco to Ho Chi Minh City, it became very clear that what is expected or valued in one culture is quite different than another. Likewise, several years ago, I moved from the mid-Atlantic region of the U.S. to the South and I soon discovered that I didn't have to be out of the country to have to learn to live differently than I had for most of my life. The fact is, when your citizenship changes, you must change as well.

Scripture tells us that we are in this world but not of it (see John 15:19). We are also instructed in Romans 12:2, **"Do not conform to the *pattern* of this world, but be transformed by the renewing of your mind. Then you will be able to test and approve what God's will is—his good, pleasing and perfect will" (NIV).** Ezekiel 11:12 says, **"And you will know that I am the LORD, for you have not followed my decrees or kept my laws but have conformed to the *standards* of the nations around you" (NIV).** These Scriptures and others make it clear that the culture of the kingdom is different than that of the world. It's clear that we are expected to cease to live and do things in the way that those who are of the world would. This need to live according to the ways of the kingdom is becoming more and more necessary. Even many who attend church regularly have begun to accept ideas and behaviors that are in direct opposition to the teachings of Jesus. We are in a time when evil is being called good and good is being called evil. Those who have chosen to follow Jesus are, more than ever before, strangers living in a foreign land.

In the natural, we can learn the local colloquialisms and develop a taste for foods which we have not eaten before. We can even learn to drive on the opposite side of the road or feign the appropriate accent. But the kingdom and kingdom education is not about our natural citizenship, but our spiritual citizenship and its reflection in the way we live in the natural. We are kingdom dwellers and we serve the King of kings. It is this truth that necessitates ensuring that students are learning to be good kingdom citizens and are being prepared to take the rule and the reign of King Jesus throughout the earth. It bears repeating—Comenius School's foundation to building impactful, world changing, God glorifying, kingdom reigning, young people is chapel. We must settle it in our own minds that this truth is a kingdom school's top priority. Then we can begin the work of kingdom education.

Hopefully, I have established the point that chapel is a very necessary starting point in kingdom schools, but it is precisely that—a starting point. The goal would be to start here and allow what transpires in chapel to fuel and inspire the rest of the day. If chapel is key to facilitating and sustaining a kingdom approach to education, then it is certainly reasonable that much prayer, thought, and planning be done in advance to create a welcoming and inviting place for the Lord to come. If encountering Jesus is our highest priority of every chapel and everything else builds upon this, then we must do all that we can and leave the rest to the Lord.

The CSCL staff has found that it requires commitment, creativity, and courage to make the needed time and opportunities for our students to learn the ways of this new citizenship. Our daily chapel is the starting point for facilitating this transformational process. We, with great intentionality, work with Holy Spirit and with each other to engage students in an ongoing learning experience. Just as you may take French language classes or take a course to learn some of the more prevalent customs before moving to France, we view chapel as the training ground for moving from an earthly kingdom mindset and way of life to one that is indicative of God's kingdom and His culture.

The challenge is that this "in the world but not of the world" transformation cannot happen through a lifeless "chapel." Chapel must be full of God-life and be intentionally constructed in such a way as to prepare these young people for their true citizenship. These young people face the challenge of becoming a new creation and living in a different world. The analogy of the caterpillar and the butterfly is fitting. Nothing is the same. They are not the same, their environment is not the same, nor are their abilities and expectations the same. This new kingdom of which they are now a part has unfamiliar laws; the way people interact with one another ceases to be a "me first" mentality; open access to the King has been granted freely without the requirement of pomp and circumstance; the lowliest is the esteemed; the poor is made rich; the last is now first; love is no longer earned but given; there is no reason for fear, shame, or regret, for the King has made all things new; and, in this kingdom, nothing is impossible.

Some may say that all we need to do is to listen to the Holy Spirit and follow His lead and just let Him show up and change the young people. Yes, we do need to do that. But we are in a teaching and learning environment and have been charged by the Lord to prepare and equip young people. This is both an academic directive and a spiritual one. On any given day, our top priority is that we have created an environment that is conducive for encountering Jesus. Therefore, all the components that are needed to give the Holy Spirit freedom to reveal Jesus must be tended to prior to and during chapel. That, of course, includes worship that is honoring to Him. But it also should include an environment that feels safe to our students—a place where they can laugh, dance, cry, express themselves creatively, talk with someone, and feel respected and protected regardless of what they are experiencing. No student should ever feel hesitant to participate because of being concerned of what others may think or say. In order to achieve this atmosphere, we cannot just "go with the flow." This environment must be cultivated.

This past school year, I witnessed some powerful examples of building on this foundation. For instance, a major focus of our chapel has been to develop a culture of honor. We have read Scripture about it; we have prayed about it; we have found ways to facilitate that in our culture. As part of supporting the understanding of what a culture of honor is, in the Senior Bible class we had been learning how we could love the world without preaching but by doing. As part of a class project, one young man brought in a video clip from the movie *Cars*. In this clip, one of the cars made the choice to give up winning a race and instead went to the aid of another car who was struggling to make it to the finish line. After watching this short clip, we were all very moved by this story of putting someone else before yourself. The next morning, we witnessed this demonstrated in chapel completely unbeknownst to the students involved.

The day following our *Cars* clip, a young man was leading worship. He is very shy and has not made friends easily since coming to CSCL. He is also not our most accomplished musician, so for him to make the choice to take center stage as worship leader was a huge risk for him. Sometimes his worship is flawless, but there have also been times when his voice went flat and he struggled to stay on tempo. This was one of those days. He had stopped several times to replay a missed key or to clear his voice. As he sat on stage struggling, without a word to anyone, a young lady quietly got up from her seat. Without fanfare, she went to the stage and quietly pulled up a chair beside him. This young lady is a very accomplished violinist; she is truly gifted. Once seated, she softly began to tap out the tempo on her leg. She then quietly sang along with him to keep him on key. She sang so softly that only he could hear her. It was clear that she did not want to embarrass him or to take his moment from him.

The seniors who had just watched *Cars* the day before were all sitting with tears in their eyes. They got it! They saw, from the humility and encouragement given by this young lady, the truth of being self-sacrificing and putting others before yourself. The fact is, she could have taken the stage at any point and would have received enthusiastic applause in appreciation for her musical gift. She chose, however, to be invisible and to support a classmate so that he could have the success that he was struggling for. Once he was finished, every student in the chapel stood and cheered. I knew they were not only cheering for the young man who didn't give up even in the face of his embarrassment, but also for the beautiful selflessness of the classmate who came to his rescue.

Another example of chapel training and learning to live in the kingdom is in the area of prayer. Students pray regularly as part of our daily chapel. They will pray for each other, families, CSCL, staff, ministry leadership, and local and world events. This past year, God has given us a new focus on fasting and intercession. Much time has been devoted in chapel and elsewhere to help students learn to engage God in a way that is sacrificial on their part, but brings a higher level of freedom and impact for the individual and for the kingdom.

A young man shared about his first experience with intercession. As a result of it being a focus in chapel, he determined to intercede uninterrupted for 30 minutes. He said that although it was difficult in the beginning, once he started, he didn't want to stop. During this time of intercession, he felt strong impressions of his grandfather who had died a couple of years prior. He had loved him very much and felt the pain of his loss ever since. While interceding, he felt a strong presence of the Lord and began to weep. When the weeping ceased, he stopped interceding, only to realize that the intercession had been for him. He has since shared that he no longer feels the heartache of losing his grandfather. He now remembers his grandfather lovingly and looks forward to seeing him again in heaven.

Chapel impacts the CSCL atmosphere and staff and students' lives daily. It is quite an amazing experience to have a 1st grader stop you in the hallway because the Holy Spirit told them to pray for you. I have heard accounts of 3rd graders learning how to extend forgiveness to one another and new friendships being formed. One class is learning the power of their words and are making declarations over themselves and their fellow classmates. Few things have touched me as much as watching the simple faith of a child as our lower school students move about the chapel to give prophetic words to upper school students, guest speakers, or staff, demonstrating humility and fearlessness. It is evident they are learning the ways of the kingdom and adapting to their citizenship there.

Many of our upper school students have come to place very high value on daily chapel. When asked to give feedback on their chapel experience, one student stated that the student led aspect had been their favorite part. They said, "For me, that is what has elicited the most value in my spiritual experience— seeing my classmates and friends seeking after God and the changes it has brought in their lives. My favorite times have been when students have openly shared testimonies or struggles. That openness and vulnerability is a catalyst for breakthrough."

Another student expressed how they had come to take chapel for granted. But when they moved from the area and the student was away from CSCL, they found themself longing for the intimacy, both with God and with the school family they had known prior. When they returned to CSCL a year later, they had a new appreciation for the school and particularly for chapel. This student felt that chapel was vital to the character of the school and stated that it was the "highlight" of their day.

Another young man attributes chapel with his ability to make choices that kept him on track with God. He said, "Chapel has instilled in me the worth of spending time with the Lord. Because of the times that I have encountered the Lord's presence during chapel, my mindset and my lifestyle have changed." And another young man said, "I love that we can start each day off with worship. I have seen many miracles in chapel as God moved. Guest speakers have brought impactful, life-changing words or a fresh perspective on life. Chapel has taught me to live a lifestyle of worship and prayer. Morning chapel has given me a firm foundation and has allowed me to develop faith and courage to do that which God puts on my heart to do, sometimes even if no one else will do them."

When seniors were asked recently to give a testimony regarding their own chapel experience, one student expressed it this way: "One of the unique qualities of CSCL is its sense of importance in creating an atmosphere for students to connect with God through prayer and worship. After attending other Christian schools, my first year at Comenius was a breath of fresh air. Now after four years, the chapel scene is often electric. God moves, and both the staff and students are changed. Most of us come every day ready to receive more... I have seen students who were passionate about trying new ways to worship God through music, but other expressions too. I have seen respect and reverence for God and the things of God. Currently, prayer is the emphasis and most God-filled aspect of our daily chapel. This year, I've seen a lot of people really open up for prayer, and I would even say that our prayer time is the center of the community in our school and is a safe place for people to be vulnerable with each other and with God."

These student testimonies are only a sampling of the role of chapel and the entirety of the kingdom learning experience. I could continue to relay story after story of students repenting, choosing to follow Jesus, miracles, answered prayer, the awe of His presence, and learning to live as citizens of the kingdom. The truth is that every staff member and every student have their story to share. I encourage you to take this journey into kingdom education with us. It is not an easy journey. We are pioneering our way to a place which most know nothing or very little about. Start at the beginning by laying your foundation with chapel.

CHAPTER 9

TEACHING IDENTITY IN THE CLASSROOM

by Julie Brown

The first thing the serpent attacked in the garden was Eve's identity. When Jesus was in the wilderness, the first thing the devil attacked was Jesus' identity. The enemy is no different today. The enemy still comes to kill, steal, and destroy—beginning with our identity. We are sons and daughters of the King of kings and Lord of lords; we are princes and princesses. The Holy Spirit works in each one of us to help us understand our identity. My important role as an educator is to partner with the Holy Spirit and with parents to raise up the next generation of kingdom-minded world changers. My goal is to work with the parents and the Holy Spirit to help each student recognize how they are made, what they believe, and why they believe it.

Developmentally, high school students are just beginning to consider who they are and what they love. Often times, our culture—even in the church—seeks to stuff individuals into a box based on how a certain age group should behave or how that age group should look. Unfortunately, this is often diametrically opposed to how the individual has been created. Therefore, as kingdom-minded educators, we must show our future world changers that they are each unique and created for a purpose far beyond what they or their circle of influence could possibly imagine. I aide my students' discovery by introducing them to a series of personality profiles, helping each student to recognize the beauty of their own individuality.

Identity Discovery Tools

What's in a Name?

At birth, each of us is given a name, usually a first and middle name followed by our surname. Each name has a meaning, and the meaning often defines who we are. In the ancient Hebrew culture, names point to the character of the child. For example, Jacob means "deceiver." He deceived his father and father-in-law. After wrestling with God, Jacob received the new name, Israel, meaning "triumphant with God" or "wrestles with God," to bless

> **Aaron G**
>
> Aaron G always assumed that his first name meant "priestly." Although this is a name of honor, he didn't believe it defined who he was or who he would become. Aaron actually means "exalted" and his middle name, Robert, means "famed, or bright and shining." Aaron G had always thought that he was created for greatness and he was invigorated to realize that his names call him to that destiny.

him and the future nation. I desire for each of my students to see the significance of their name. The first thing they do in my class is write down their first and middle name along with the meaning of each name and post them on the wall. Immediately, many of them realize that the definition of their name is prophetic. Their name either describes character traits they already possess or calls things that aren't as though they are, such as "prince" or "great one." Displaying their name and the meaning is a way of owning it and inviting other students to see who their friends are called to be. After calling out each student by their name and meaning, we move forward by taking six personality/temperament tests.

5 Love Languages Test

Using the *5 Love Languages* test[i] for teenagers helps the students begin to understand how they are loved and how to show love. The five love languages are quality time, acts of service, words of affirmation, physical touch, and gifts. Some are more easily shown in the classroom than others. Words of affirmation is one of the most popular I have found among teenagers and easily given as a teacher. Quality time, on the other hand, can be more difficult.

> **Haley**
>
> Several years ago, one of my students was struggling with family issues. We had just finished the *5 Love Languages* test a few weeks before. This particular student, Haley, needed physical touch to feel loved. We came together as a class to pray for her, but later she shared with me that when seven or eight of her classmates hugged her, that is when she felt truly loved.

Be creative. This doesn't mean as a teacher you need to spend a weekend of quality time with each student, but you might invite them to eat lunch with you once a marking period, depending on how many students you actually have. Gifts can come in the form of a piece of candy or a sticker. The gifts don't have to be expensive, only to let the students know that you are thinking of them. Physical touch, depending on the school you are in, is easy; give the infamous side hug. Acts of service is more difficult for me, but I've found asking these students what it looks like for them can help. Loving each of your students through their particular love language builds relationship. Building relationship will build trust; trust builds family and family is the kingdom. The students also begin to look at how their friends in the classroom are best loved as well, building family, which ultimately builds the kingdom.

16 Personalities Test

Next, I give them a form of the Myers-Briggs Temperament Indicator (it can be found online) called *16 Personalities Test*. This particular test gives them four letters indicating whether they are extrovert/introvert (E/I), intuitive/sensing (N/S), feeling/thinking (F/T), judging/perceiving (J/P). Initially, many of the students have misconceptions around the definitions of extrovert and introvert. They believe that an extrovert is outgoing, while an introvert is more reserved in behavior. In actuality, extroverts are those who gain energy from being around people, while introverts are those who find energy with solitude. The next set of letters, intuitive (N) or sensing (S), come from where an individual receives information. They might use either their intuition or their five senses, respectively. The third set of letters, feeling (F) versus thinking (T), describe a person's decision-making process—whether an individual relies on "gut feeling" or thinking through the problem. The final pair, judging (J) and perceiving (P), are a bit more archaic. This pair focuses on how the individual approaches life. Those who are judging prefer a more structured lifestyle, while those who are perceiving prefer a more flexible and open lifestyle. J's tend to like schedules, while P's prefer to be more spontaneous. The combination of the four tendencies produces temperaments that tend to thrive in one of four different areas: analyzing, diplomacy, guarding others, and entertainment.

After the students take the test online and read about their personality results, I ask them to post their results on the wall with their names and love languages. They also list a few bullet points that summarize the descriptions they feel best fits their personality. This encourages the students to evaluate what they know about themselves already and what they want others to know concerning who they are. Often there are several students in the same class that have the same four letters describing who they are, but they showed individuality by posting different traits. The students love to compare and contrast by telling the rest of the class how they are similar and different from one another. I encourage my fellow teachers to take the test as well. Because I know the sixteen personality types, I know that I am more likely to relate well to certain types than others; therefore, it is important for me to read about each personality to find the strength in each as I interact with each individual student. The kingdom always draws the gold from every temperament.

Whitney

Whitney is an only child. She is reserved and tends to hide from classroom discussions. When we took the *16 Personalities Test*, she was more than pleasantly surprised. Her result was ENTJ, also known as "Commander." These individuals are often "bold, imaginative, strong-willed leaders, always finding a way—or making one."

Of course, seeing herself as shy, Whitney was shocked that she was an extrovert, but what really encouraged her was learning about the other women who have the same personality type, such as Margaret Thatcher and Hillary Clinton. She actually began to cry. Whitney had never seen herself as a leader. Whitney never saw herself as strong or as someone with a voice. Whitney is now able to see herself as a world changer and a woman of influence because of the *16 Personalities Test*. https://www.16personalities.com/personality-types

The Redemptive Gifts Test

Next, I introduce the redemptive gifts found in Romans 12, using *The Redemptive Gifts* by Charles R. Wade Jr. I believe each of these gifts is given by the Father at birth. They are prophet, servant, teacher, exhorter, giver, ruler, and mercy. The book not only gives a comprehensive test at the end, but also a detailed description of each of the gifts and the traits associated with them. It amuses me that students who have similar Myers-Briggs temperaments often believe they will have the same redemptive gifts, but they are surprised when their redemptive gifts are unique and separate from their other tests. I have the students display their top two results along with several descriptors of each gift they feel best fits them. Again, I recommend teachers take the test as well to find their gifts and how they relate to those of their students.

Jack

After taking the Myers-Briggs, or *16 Personalities Test*, Jack believed he had everyone figured out. His personality was ENFP, along with eight others in his class. He then took the *Redemptive Gifts* test. He scored highest as prophet. Prophets often see things in black or white, are verbally expressive, are extremely opinionated, and are visionaries. Many of these lineup with ENFPs.

Jack, in prophet fashion, vocalize that he believed that the other eight ENFPs were probably prophets as well, but he was wrong. Only one of them had the prophet gift. In fact, several of them were the opposite—mercy. A person with a mercy gift usually works as a peacemaker; they hate confrontation and enjoy listening to others more than speaking. Jack, as well as the rest of the class, quickly learned that just because they are similar in some areas does not mean they will be similar in all areas.

DISC Test

The DISC test is the next test I suggest. As with the redemptive gifts, I ask the students to post their top two results with a few bullet points describing how the test best explains their individual traits. The definitions vary for what each letter stands for, but I usually adhere to the following: D – dominant, I – influencer, S – steady, and C – conscientious. Those with the dominant (D) personality type are usually outgoing and task-oriented. They seem to be focused on problem solving, results, and the bottom line. A great example is President Donald Trump. Those with the influencer (I) personality type are usually outgoing and people-oriented. They focus on drawing attention with a purpose and interacting with people. An example of the influencer is President Bill Clinton. Those with the steady (S) personality type are usually reserved and people oriented. They seem to be focused on preserving relationships and maintaining peace and harmony. A strong example of the steady personality type was Mother Teresa. Finally, those with conscientious (C)

Aiden

Personally, I rank highly in both D (dominant) and I (influencer). My strengths from these two temperament types allow me to both work well with tasks and with people. I see the big picture and can command those around me with diplomacy. Unfortunately, I have very little C (conscientious) in me at all; therefore, I have trouble with the details. I learned several years ago to partner with people to cover this weakness.

Aiden is a strong C. He is the perfect intern for me. Of course, as an English teacher, I grade paper, after paper, after paper. Aiden grades the grammar and punctuation that I miss. He also recognizes misspelled words when I don't. This is an example of how you can focus on your strengths and ask for help to cover your weaknesses.

personalities are usually reserved and task-oriented. They are focused on details, facts, and rules. A great example for this personality type was Albert Einstein.

As the teacher and students take this personality profile, I highly recommend finding an online chart showing the strengths and weaknesses of each personality type displaying it. It is at this point that I begin to encourage the students to look at their strengths, but also consider their weaknesses. There is great value in focusing on and developing our strengths to their potential. It is counterproductive to focus too much on our weaknesses; however, I do consider my weaknesses so that I can surround myself with others who have strengths that can cover my weaknesses. I use the DISC test to encourage my students to do the same.

Enneagram Test

I have recently added the *Enneagram* test to my classroom[ii]. The *Enneagram* test determines one of nine distinct personality types. This test considers the dominant personality type you are born with, but also how a personality can be altered by adapting to other's personalities. With this consideration, the Enneagram test also classifies the level of health of a personality as either healthy, average, or unhealthy. With this particular test, I recommend teachers study and evaluate the *Enneagram* before taking it and have students do the same. Again, this profile is new to my repertoire, and I am learning how to best use this in my classroom, but I am finding that it can be the most rewarding test to promote personal growth.

Strength Finders 2.0

Strength Finders 2.0 is the final personality test I give; it is also my favorite. Gallup introduced the thirty-four strengths, suggesting that too often our natural talents and strengths go untapped. I require the students to read the first section of the book before taking the test online. This introduces how *Strength Finders* works and encourages the reader to focus on their strengths and the suggestions given in their results. These results give each individual their top five strengths as well as how these strengths work together. The students again post their results with several bullet points describing each strength. They enjoy the individuality described by this particular survey. Rarely do any of them have more than two strengths that are matched by anyone else in the class, and they are almost never in the same order.

Karen

Karen is an international student. She comes from a culture where both men and women are expected to be reserved. She continually struggles to comply with her cultural norms and is often at odds with her parents because of this. In the first few weeks of school, Karen would often come to me crying because she didn't feel like she fit in to any community or culture.

One of Karen's top five strengths from *Strength Finders 2.0* is WOO, also known as Winning Others Over. People exceptionally talented in the WOO theme love the challenge of meeting new people, breaking the ice, and connecting with them. Karen, like many other WOOs, often has high energy that draws others to her.

After realizing that Winning Others Over is a strength instead of a weakness, Karen has begun to feel as though she has permission to be who she is created to be. The *Strength Finders 2.0* test and results gave Karen a sense of freedom.

Class Structure of Profiles

I begin the first day of class with the name and meaning research, followed by the love languages test. The rest of the profiles are interspersed throughout the remainder of the curriculum. I typically give a personality profile test at the end of a unit, giving the students some relaxation time before beginning the next unit. Sometimes, though, the Holy Spirit guides me to give one earlier or later, depending on how the class is growing in identity.

Ultimately, the Holy Spirit is the only one who can truly show any of us who we are, but these different assessments can help change the way we look at ourselves and the world around us. They can give us strategies to better understand how we have been individually created to bring the kingdoms of this world into the kingdom.

Believe Discovery Tools

These personality profiles and tests help each student discover their identity and how they were uniquely created, but it is almost equally important for them to understand what they believe and why. I teach 11th and 12th graders for the most part; I understand that my students are entering the "real world" after they leave my class. Many of them will be headed to secular universities, some to a secular school for the first time. In recent years, our university systems have begun teaching our students "what to think" instead of "how to think." Therefore, I want my students to learn how to think before they graduate.

Fortunately, I teach literature, language, and composition, which is a subject that easily opens the door to controversial themes, ripe for discussion; however, almost any subject matter or class has opportunity for discussion. I see my position as more of a facilitator or coach for each discussion. I have the opportunity and privilege to ask the difficult questions, while my students' receive input from parents, family, and school have the opportunity and privilege to learn how to think for themselves. Up to this point in their lives, many of them have church and their community which has shaped and molded their belief systems. It is imperative that they begin to synthesize what they have learned from others into their own convictions.

In class, we take a topic, concept, or theme found in the literature we are reading, and I simply ask the students what they think. I stay quiet and allow the students to discuss the topic among themselves. I suggest that you have the desk or classroom set in a circle or semicircle to promote discussion so each student can see the faces of the rest of the class. The teacher also needs to make sure that each student has the opportunity to vocalize their opinion. If you have some that are more shy than others, ask the more reserved ones to speak before those who more freely voice their opinions. The students should also give their reasons why they believe or feel as they do. If they do not

---

Student Voice

As in most schools, our students experience frustrations about administrative decisions that are out of their control. Last year, I sat down with a group of twenty 10th grade students to hear their frustrations. All I did was ask them their opinion on the situation. For the next hour, every one of the students in the group voiced their concerns. They were thankful that I allowed them a voice. They told me the truth and did not pull punches. They were not dishonorable. They just wanted to be heard.

It is important for educators to remember to listen to our students, no matter what their age or abilities. They are still people, and people need a voice.

---

know how to answer the question, then I require them to find evidence to support their opinion. Later in the conversation, I give them my own opinion and support. I make it clear that they do not have to agree with me, as long as they understand their own belief systems and can support them. This makes the classroom safe. If the classroom is not safe, the students will not listen, learn, or seek to understand the teacher or other students.

Summary

Promoting identity promotes the kingdom. I want my students to leave my class with more than just head knowledge. It is imperative that they have some comprehension of who they are and what they believe. This sometimes means setting my prepared lesson plans aside for the day. The kingdom is more important than the curriculum. The most important guide as a kingdom educator is the Holy Spirit. My job is to stay connected with Him, invite Him into my classroom every morning, and trust that He is leading me in what I teach, facilitate, coach, and impart.

Davis

As an 11th and 12th grade English teacher, I love having the students who have been a part of CSCL since kindergarten. They are usually more comfortable in their skin than others. At the same time, I love having the new students come into our culture who were raised in the public school system. These new students seem a little off-balance at the beginning of their time in our school. One such student, Davis*, came to us from a large public high school that had a less than fabulous reputation.

Davis started a week into the school year, knowing only one or two students at CSCL. I could tell he was a little nervous, and I asked him if he would like to sit in the desk closest to me. He quickly took me up on my offer. As we began taking personality tests in the class, I could tell he was a little uncomfortable. This discomfort continued and heightened as I asked the students to journal what they thought about certain topics and themes we were reading in literature. Then, when I requested that Davis share his thoughts, he turned to me and quietly said, "Mrs. Brown you want me to know who I am and what I believe? I am used to walking in class, picking up several worksheets, going to the back of the room, sitting down, completing those worksheet, and turning them in when the bell rings."

I replied, "Davis, if you do not know who you are or what you believe by the time you graduate, then I'm afraid that this world might chew you up and spit you out."

Over the next few months, Davis went from a shy young man who did not want to talk in my class, to standing on stage before a crowd and hosting our school talent show. He continues to amaze me as a growing leader, both spiritually and in the classroom.

Frankenstein

I love teaching *Frankenstein*. The book is full of themes and motifs that often ignite passionate classroom discussions. One such discussion centers on personal choice. I ask the students whether or not the monster or Victor Frankenstein was responsible for the monster's decisions. My goal is for the students to begin to take ownership for their actions, despite how others have treated them, but I do not begin with that statement.

The students choose a side and gather on one side of the room or the other, depending on their opinion. Their goal is to persuade everyone on the other side of the room that their group decision is the correct one. Each person in the group presents their reasons, and I act as moderator only.

In my most recent class, it took an hour and a half for everyone to share and pick a final side. At the end of class, all but one of the students believed that the monster was responsible for his own decisions. As they debriefed, they all realized they are responsible for their own actions, no matter the behavior or influence of those around them. More importantly, they understood what they believed and why.

[i]Test for teenagers can be found at www.5lovelanguages.com/profile/teens.
[ii]I encourage teachers to study this profile at https://www.enneagraminstitute.com/ before taking the test or assigning it to their students.

CHAPTER 10

THE CREATIVE CLASSROOM: ART AT CSCL

by Dawn Hartigan

I've been told that when an artist goes to heaven, they will have a studio in their mansion, full of every possible material and tool imaginable. We will even be painting with light! However, here on earth, specifically in my classroom, we make use of everything and improvise a lot. We recycle, reuse, repurpose, and restore, just like the Lord does with us. My main focus is to impart skills to my students so they are able to express themselves visually. Not every student will become an artist, but each one has creativity put in them by God. It's my job to help them figure out how to express their unique gift.

By building skill sets with children, frustration can be avoided in their art making. For example, many children in kindergarten and 1st grade are learning how to use scissors and glue sticks. They are learning how to draw shapes for the first time. An excellent art lesson will include skill-building in these areas, as well as introduce an artist, an art movement, or a specific process like painting, printmaking, or weaving. I have set up my curriculum to cover certain skills and medium (materials) each month. I also focus on an artist, a movement in art history, or a technique.

Introducing Skills

To introduce or practice cutting with scissors, using a glue stick, and drawing shapes, we might look at Wassily Kandinski's painting *Color Study, Squares with Concentric Circles* (1913). I ask the student what they see going on in the painting. We talk about what a concentric circle is and try to guess how Kandinsky might have painted this painting.

To begin, students cut the smallest circle first from a piece of colored construction paper. This small circle is glued to another, larger piece of construction paper. Now the student cuts a larger concentric circle around the first circle. They repeat this until they have a circle with many different colored rings. It is then glued to a large piece of background paper.

I have these specific goals in mind:

1. Cut concentric circles freehand

2. Use a glue stick properly

3. Learn about Kandinsky's work

4. Create a pleasing composition

Even though I have these goals in mind, the students have many choices to make on their own. They choose what colors they want to put together, how big they want to make their circles, and where to arrange them on the paper. Some students will draw a grid and place their circles inside squares just like Kandinsky. Others will randomly place them all over the background, sometimes overlapping them. Because they are given the freedom to make these choices, each art work is unique and reflects the child's preferences for color and design.

I also want each person to be engaged and to feel successful. If they are struggling to cut a circle out freehand, I suggest that they draw a circle first and then cut it out. If this is still too hard, we look for something to trace. When I use this lesson with preschool children, I cut circles and let them glue them together. This same work of art can be used to teach a lesson on color mixing with tempera paint or oil pastels. Each material has different strengths and challenges.

Working with "Mistakes"

I love art; I always have. However, I have met students who really struggle and don't enjoy the idea of having to push themselves past their negative beliefs about art. Some of those lies are "You have to be born with artistic talent." Though talent helps, practice and perseverance are more important. Another lie is "Artists can't make a living, so I'll be a doctor." Many creative people are making a substantial living doing what they love. It's more about passion and working towards a goal. "I don't have any ideas!" Then copy something until you get one. Of course my all-time favorite, "I can't draw a straight line to save my life!" Really? Here's a ruler.

The fear of failure is really the fear of man. Instead of letting children crumple up their paper, I ask them to work with their "mistake" or use the back side of the paper. This is not a hard and fast rule, but you can't let students feel like it has to look like the teacher's sample or to be right. The book *Beautiful Oops!*

by Barney Saltzberg is great to encourage children, young and old, to see their "oops" as an opportunity to create something surprising. To reinforce this idea, I save all "mistakes" and put them in the "oops box." We take this box out, and students can use other people's "oops" to make something new by collaging bits of the "mistake" papers onto a background.

Creating an Art Notebook

Art notebooks are a tool I use to develop skills and teach concepts in the 4th and 5th grade. These books are handmade by the students and are used to explore the Elements of Art (color, line, shape, value, space, form, and texture) and Principle of Design (rhythm, proportion, emphasis, variety, unity, repetition, pattern, and movement). Students create a cover, a title page, and many two-page spreads. The two-page spreads focus on a skill or technique used by a famous artist. The student does art work using the techniques that emulate the artist.

For example, when studying the element of line, we look at the paintings by Piet Mondrian, which are grids made from black lines and shapes that are filled in with the three primary colors (red, blue, yellow) and white. On the left page, students draw their initials in block letters and use patterns to fill them. They write notes about the artist at the bottom of the page. The right page is where students create their own art work, using lines to draw a grid and fill in the shapes with red, yellow, and blue markers. At the bottom of this page, students glue a picture of Piet Mondrian and one of his works of art. The last step is to title their art work and write one or two sentences about the artist or their art work.

Making their own art notebook is fun and rewarding. It is an investment of time and effort on the student's part and most likely will not be thrown away. It also avoids a lot of loose papers going home, crumpled up in a backpack.

To make your art notebook you will need:

- 1 sheet of Bristol board 12 x 18" per book

- 8 sheets of 12 x 18" 80lb. drawing paper

- Awl, book binding thread, and needles or a long-reach stapler

- Duct Tape

To construct the booklet:

1. Paint, stencil, stamp etc. 1 sheet of 12 x 18" Bristol board for the cover and let it dry completely. Use waterproof materials if possible.

2. Take 8 sheets of paper per book and fold each sheet in half to 9"x12", cradling one sheet inside the next, until they are all stacked up. This will give you 32 sides, counting the front and back of each sheet.

3. Fold the cover in half and place the pages inside. If stapling the book, staple so the staples are smooth on the inside center of the book and skip to step 6.

4. If you are going to sew the book together, use the awl to make holes at 1", 2.5", 4", 5.5", 7", 8.5", and 10" through all thicknesses.

5. Sew the pages together, tying the ends together in a double knot.

6. Cut a piece of duct tape 14" long.

7. With the book facedown so the rough edges of the staples or sowing are showing, use the duct tape to reinforce the binding on the cover and to cover the stapes or stiches. If you opted to sew the binding, make sure to tuck the string in under the duct tape.

Using the Bristol board as a cover costs a little more, but it is much more durable than construction paper. By using an 80lb paper, you will be able to use wet medium in the book. Sharpies do bleed through, however, so keep that in mind. I also have used 140lb water color paper and glued that into the book for special projects like plein air painting with watercolors. The current cost for these books is under $1.50.

The art notebooks build confidence in students as they complete each two-page spread. Students who may have felt intimidated at first, feel proud of completing their projects. This confidence reinforces the truth that practice, not just talent, really does make a difference. One of my high school students expressed misgivings about art. After making her notebook, she felt that she really did have artistic ability. She had changed her "I am not creative" statement about herself to, "I am pretty good at this aren't I?" Awakening this creative spirit in people is so important.

Introducing Art Vocabulary

Art, like any subject, has its own vocabulary. Even young children can learn basic color theory terms when presented in a fun lesson. This vocabulary helps them discuss their own artwork as well as great works of art by other artists. To teach about cool and warm colors, two terms used when talking about color, I use a lesson based on Jim Dine's painting, *Four Hearts* (1969). The first graders were asked to choose either warm colors (red, yellow, orange) or cool colors (green, blue, purple) to make their hearts. One first graders exclaimed, "I want my heart to be warm because I want a happy heart! I don't want to make sad hearts!" He made a connection between the idea of warm and cool colors and how they can express emotion.

Because art is a visual language, a person's thoughts, emotions, and experiences are present in their work. God can speak through anyone's artwork. As Christian artists, we are trying to express what we sense God is saying. We may be trying to share an actual vision or dream we've received from the Lord. My goal as an art teacher is to help children express those things so others can benefit from what they are receiving from the Lord.

Introducing Getting Ideas

After I've spent 10-12 weeks teaching skills, I move the 4th and 5th grade classes toward TAB, Teaching for Artistic Behavior (http://teachingforartisticbehavior.org). This is a relatively new idea in art education that is training students to think like an artist. I begin by showing them some of my own work and asking them, "Where do artists get their ideas?" At first most students can't answer this question. They think artists miraculously get ideas and just make art. I tell them this is not true.

Students who are already making art outside of class may be able to answer this question. We talk about how artists get inspired by looking at art done by other artists; reading books, internet articles, and blogs; and reviewing magazines about art. I show them examples of some of my favorite art books, magazines, and blogs. Inspiration comes from many places. We also talk about going to art shows and museums to view art. Knowing that an artist has to look for ideas really helps students feel they can be an artist too.

Next, we cover what reference materials are and where to find them. Because students are used to being given instruction and materials to complete projects, they may not know where or how to find reference materials. Reference materials may come from life—such as an apple or orange from the refrigerator. Or you might need a photograph of a lion, since a real-life lion would not be a good idea in the classroom. However, going to the zoo to draw from life would be awesome!

Students need to be trained how to gather the reference information they need to create something that is all their idea. This is a good time to talk about the difference between copying for practice and plagiarism. Artists can get permission to copy a work of art in a museum, but they can never say that it is their original idea and design. An artist must copy in order to become skilled, but eventually they develop their own style and ideas.

Finally, we discuss the medium available in the art room. By now, they should have had a chance to use all the 2D materials, such as pencils, markers, oil pastels, and colored pencils. They have also used watercolor, tempera, and acrylic paint in their notebooks. Students should know where they are stored and how to care for them. Respecting art materials, conserving materials, and keeping the art room clean and in order are good habits. I once had a professor who said every artist's workspace should be as orderly as a surgeon's operating room. That, of course, was his opinion. However, I do think it is helpful for students to always know where to find supplies and return them. This cuts down on me having to set up and clean up.

Setting Up the Art Room

The art room is set up into centers. Each center is focused on certain technique. There is a drawing, a painting, a collage, and a 3D center. Outside is an observation and mess making center. Other centers that rotate in and out are weaving, jewelry making, and a building center using Legos and other building materials. I limit each center to two to four students, depending on the projects and the space needed to work comfortably. Students are allowed to work in a center for two to three weeks at a time. If no one else is interested in that center, a student can stay longer. Each student fills out a planning sheet for me. Here are the questions they fill out.

What is your idea?

What reference materials do you need?

What medium will you use?

Sketch out your idea.

Get Mrs. Hartigan (the teacher) to ok your project.

Eventually, all the planning should be taking place at home. Students should come in with all the reference materials they will need and any supplies that we don't have in the classroom. They walk in focused and stay that way because they are choosing what to work on, instead of having all the decisions made for them. This planning stage will eventually move into a visual journal format. A visual journal is different from a sketchbook, because it is not just sketches. It includes inspirations, doodles, words, pictures, and experiments. It is a visual diary for planning projects and recording inspiration (see more at http://www.visualjournaling.com).

Learning Art Critique

Once a month, we take time to reflect on what each student has been working on. We talk about what they learned as well as what worked and what didn't. This is a good time for peer teaching and coaching. Students learn to view other people's art and give positive, constructive critiques. They also learn to receive suggestions and to verbalize their thought processes.

Finally, they learn to write artist statements. These statements are placed with the work they exhibit during art shows.

God is the Creator. He is our never-ending source of witty ideas and creativity. Teaching students how to use their creative gifts to honor God and serve His people is my greatest honor. I believe each of us has a creative gift from the Lord that may be just waiting to come out. Pick up a crayon, a paintbrush, bake a gourmet meal, invent a new product, or build something. I tell my students, "Bless the Lord by using the gifts He's put inside of you!"

CHAPTER 11

FUEL FOR LEARNING

by Ximena Gonzalez

For years, the education system has been told what to do and how to do it. The teaching and learning process has been locked in the square of the classroom, and we limit education by withholding passion and expression of individuality. Kingdom education unlocks the classroom and provides an open space where creativity takes place, ideas are birthed, and projects rise from every student with the support of their teachers.

"Develop a passion for learning. If you do, you will never cease to grow." - Anthony J. D'Angelo

Interest and passion are the place where inspiration, motivation, and focus bloom. When one is passionate about things that interest them, they are willing to invest time and self-discipline to achieve goals. I teach high school Spanish, and I focus on teaching from my students' places of passion and interests.

Presentations of Passion

I like to encourage my students to share their passions and dreams with the whole class. I have found that they are engaged by their own insights and become interested in expanding their ideas when they are passionate about the topic.

The development of their interest, motivated by a focused passion, produces creative ideas. During our Spanish class, I incorporated a Spanish presentation of entrepreneurial projects from the students' interests and skills. I found that my students were considerably motivated to share their projects and to contribute to their classmates' ideas.

Emanuel composed his Spanish presentation about his ideas for ecological architecture, which uses natural energy solutions in the building design. He made a presentation with unique building plans he created for modern house designs. His classmates were curious about how everything worked in the various rooms of the house, so in order to participate and give him advice, they went to our textbook, where we had studied about the parts of a house, and practiced the new vocabulary with their comments and questions about the ecological aspects of each room.

Charles shared with us his passion for soccer, introducing his favorite soccer players and teams. Of course, every soccer fan in the classroom had an opinion or comment on this topic. His project proposal was about creating his own soccer academy. The students were excited to give him some suggestions and voice their own opinions and, once again, they were challenged to communicate their ideas in Spanish.

Hanna loves healthy food. Her entrepreneurial idea for her presentation was about running healthy food trucks. Her presentation focused on the best locations and cities for food trucks as well as the benefits for busy people to eat healthy food instead of fast food. This was a great presentation because the students had to look up vocabulary for cities, locations, and food all for the same topic.

I apply this same principle when we are learning vocabulary about professions. I asked my students to share with everyone the abilities, skills, and talents they already have and what professions work well with their skills. They had creative ideas about their future jobs and businesses that they were excited to share. Once again, their interests were engaged and they learned a great deal of vocabulary to explain their skills and talents and how they fit a certain profession. One student, Mackenzie, shared with us her skills and talents, and she mentioned she was passionate about photography, painting, and clothing design. Right away, her classmates started telling her how to connect her gifts with her own future business. We encouraged her to start creating a draft of a catalog and share it with us as a project. She was truly motivated by her passion, and her final presentation was outstanding. She ended the semester with a presentation about her future magazine, what it would be named, how it would look, and an agenda of things to do to begin stepping forward into her passion.

These presentations were interactive because the students were passionate about the topic. We could have easily used textbook examples for presentations, but those ideas belong to someone else who thought they would work well inside the classroom. It is more effective when we use textbooks creatively as helpers and not dictators of our class. When the students started thinking of their passions outside of the classroom, we had original ideas that stretched each student to find the right words to use.

Be Passionate Yourself

As part of the presentations on their passions and interests, one day a student shared his passion for graphic design. He introduced a new type of technology for graphic design that I had not heard of before, and I realized it could be used in my own advertisements in the marketing world. I have a dream of having a coffee shop one day, and I shared with the class my dream, explaining that this type of graphic design would help me with my future coffee shop. Within seconds, everybody was raising their hands to suggest their own ideas to help me with my coffee shop. They gave me a variety of things to consider, ranging from how to make their favorite espresso to the name and kind of flowers that I should have in front of my shop. It is amazing how detailed and thoughtful their advice was, even as they were looking up Spanish words to explain their ideas. It was an encouragement to me to see the students apply their own creativity and passions in combination with the vocabulary we learned in class. This is a perfect example of kingdom education. Instead of focusing only on learning inside the classroom and from generic lessons, I found a way to expand their education into their dreams about their future and even my future.

As teachers, we can provoke our students' creativity by sharing with them what we are passionate about. I would suggest every teacher to reflect on what they truly like and be open to express it before the class. It is an interesting way to encourage the students' participation and ideas. Once the students realize that their teachers have their own goals and desires, the students become more willing to share their personal goals and passions. As teachers, we can encourage their goals and connect them to our class subjects, especially when we are open to sharing about our own goals. This opens up the possibilities and encourages our students to remain engaged and motivated.

God and Passions

In my Spanish class, we also found several ways to grow our relationship with God. My favorite kingdom action is having the students learn how to say kind words to each other in Spanish. There is a genuine expression of friendship among the students when they can build each other up and focus on encouraging the best in their unique personalities. I learned that they can be truly authentic and beautifully vulnerable. Students practiced saying their kind words in Spanish, which eventually extended their adjectives and vocabulary in our target language. This works great as an icebreaker in the classroom, starting each day with learning how to say encouraging and kind words to each other. Whether you teach a foreign language or any other subject, this activation will positively affect your teaching environment.

As a class, we also found a way to make a constant correlation between the materials presented in class and Jesus' lifestyle or other stories and characters from the Bible. Kingdom culture does not force the student's relationship with God, but cultivates it by encouraging them through biblical principles and examples. During our Spanish class, one of the first grammar lessons I teach is how to use and conjugate adjectives connected to the masculine and feminine pronouns. After explaining to my students the grammar structures, we practiced describing each other. If we were in a typical Spanish classroom, the textbook would focus on describing physical characteristics of people pictured in a book, but kingdom education is about making personal connections and being creative. We came up with an exercise to reflect on how the Bible describes us. Each student found adjectives that described who we are in Christ, and we found that we are described as royal priests, kingdom ambassadors, a new creation, more than conquerors, a city on a hill, a holy nation, and so much more. With this simple exercise, our class was not only practicing and learning new vocabulary, but also reflecting on our identity in Christ.

There is no limit for creativity when students can express their passions, develop their interests, and encourage each other to be who God has made them to be. It is truly important to keep in mind as an educator that the first student in the classroom is always the teacher, so we must have our own passions and interests. Kingdom education helps the students to think beyond just what happens within the four walls of the classroom, and instead to expand their vision into their own future, and even the future of the teacher, so they can pursue their passions creatively.

> *The proper education of the young does not consist in stuffing their heads with a mass of words, sentences, and ideas dragged together out of various authors, but in opening up their understanding to the outer world, so that a living stream may flow from their own minds, just as leaves, flowers, and fruit spring from the bud on a tree.*
>
> *- John Amos Comenius*

CHAPTER 12

SPIRITUAL INTELLIGENCE OPERATIONS

by Marcia Rensink

Introduction

We can equip students to connect with God in their hearts, not just their heads. Romans 10:10 says, **"For with the heart one believes" (NKJV).** The Greek word for "heart" in the New Testament rarely refers to the physical organ. Instead, it refers to "the center of the inner life of man and the source or seat of all forces and functions of soul and spirit."[1] The Hebrew mindset sees the heart as an "operating force" that can stir us up and cause actions from the will.[2] Students coming from Christian families know right from wrong, but usually don't know how to connect to God in their innermost being. We can demonstrate through simple steps to practice how to make this connection. Just as we learn to reason with our minds, we can learn to discern through our innermost being. The world is experienced first through the mind, but the Spirit is experienced first from within. Scripture often calls this internal place as "the belly." In John 7:37-38, Jesus boldly proclaims that a drink from Jesus becomes a river that flows out of the belly. Our belly is the first point where emotions are felt. Just take a minute to stop and focus on your innermost being or belly. Now think of your most joyful experience. Did you feel the lift? Try something that makes you afraid. Do you feel the difference? Our belly is the barometer of our innermost being or spiritual heart. Proverbs 20:27 says, **"The spirit of man is the candle of the Lord, searching all the inward parts of the belly" (AKJV).** Our sensitivity to the Holy Spirit is primarily felt through the belly, not the mind. The mind just helps us decode His promptings. Discernment from the Holy Spirit by becoming sensitive to your belly is a skill that needs to be taught and practiced, otherwise students revert to logic and reason alone.

Operations of the Human Spirit

While connected to our Source and Creator, there are several basic operations that are exercised by the human spirit. These operations are necessary for spiritual maturity, discernment, and battle. The basic operations that we can do to develop are spirit are receiving, releasing, and forgiving.[3] Developing a sensitivity and attentiveness to the operating of the Holy Spirit is pivotal to fully function in any spiritual operation.

Sensitivity and Attentiveness

Students are able to develop their sensitivity as they grow in awareness of Christ within and they build relationship with the Holy Spirit. Bible reading and prayer are taught as spiritual disciplines, but they become encounters when the spirit is stirred (see Luke 24:32). Graham Cooke says it this way: "There is an indwelling presence of the Holy Spirit. It's quiet, it's purposeful. It's almost like a behind the scenes thing, but you've got to pay attention to it."[4] Recognizing the inner stirring of the Holy Spirit is the ground floor of growing in sensitivity. If students have not accepted Christ as Lord and Savior, these exercises will be of little interest. Add these students to your prayer list and offer opportunities for accepting Christ, but don't discount the value of this training for them for later in their spiritual journey. Those who have experienced an encounter with Christ will be able to cooperate more completely with the Holy Spirit.

Attentiveness is developed by learning how to recognize emotions with both positive and negative indicators.

- Positive indicators: peace, joy, compassion, love, wholeness, fulfillment

- Negative indicators: anxiety, fear, sadness, lust, anger, guilt, shame, pride

Sensitivity and attentiveness are skills that need to be developed. We long to receive in our innermost being, for our spirit to be alive, but do we regularly open our spirits to commune with God? We are commanded to "worship in spirit and in truth." How do we worship with our spirit? Here are some practical steps to become sensitive to your spirit and the Holy Spirit working in you.

Steps to discerning in your spirit:

1. Focus on the innermost being or belly area. Do the exercise where you feel different emotions. Think of a time when you opened your best present what do you feel in your belly? Do ten different emotions.

2. Learn to recognize emotions in the belly and respond properly to them. Negative emotions (sadness, fear, lust, anger, guilt and shame) and positive emotions (love, joy, peace, patience, kindness, goodness, faithfulness,

gentleness, self-control). This takes practice because we tend to go to the mind first. Since negative emotions are basically stepping into the enemy's camp, we handle these through forgiveness or release.

3. Learn to yield to Christ, just as you did when you accepted Him as your Savior (see Colossians 2:6). My yielding to Christ was "I give up, I don't want to try to be good enough anymore, I need You." Start by acting out situations where yielding happens, you say "OK," "I give up," "yes," "I'll do it," or heave a big sigh while focusing on how it feels in the belly.

4. Learn to grow and maintain the positive emotions, especially peace. Notice when peace leaves. As you grow in awareness of peace, this is stepping into discernment.

5. Learn to ask God "yes and no" questions and read the peace in your belly.

God equipped our bodies to inform our mind so we can understand what is going on in our spirit. We must pay attention to our bodies. What you believe in your heart rules over your mind.

Basic Operation: Receive

When we learn the basic operation of receiving, it is also facilitated through the spiritual inward being or the belly. For younger students, you can have them visualize a door on their belly that they open. This is yielding to God, a surrender of the will. For older students, remind them of their conversion experience (see Colossians 2:6). Just as you received Christ, now receive other things from Him—love, strength, joy, compassion, and grace. Grace is not only God's unmerited favor.

Grace is God empowering us to do His will. II Corinthians 9:8 proclaims, **"God is able to make all grace abound toward you, that you always having all sufficiency in all things, may have an abundance for every good work."** God gave His grace to Jesus, the apostles, and the churches of Macedonia (see Luke 2:40, Acts 4:33, II Corinthians 8:1-7). If they needed grace, so do we. II Peter 3:18 commands us to grow in grace. This exercise will help you grow in grace.

> EXERCISE: This is a simple exercise of asking for God's grace (His empowering) to meet whatever comes your way.
>
> - Relax and focus on Jesus inside you (using the belly as the focal point).
>
> - As an act of your will, let God know you surrender to Him (open the door).
>
> - Physically position your open hands next to or on your belly.
>
> - Say out loud, "Father, I ask for and receive Your grace for today."[6]

This could be done daily as part of a devotional time. When you do this exercise with your students, follow up by asking if anyone noticed a difference in their day. I did this with my students, and one testimony I heard was from Jane. She told me she was able to keep her cool when someone approached her ready to argue, and the argument was avoided. She felt God empowering her and was actually able to redirect the conversation to the root of the argument and suggest a solution. They resolved the argument and left friends.

Basic Operation: Release

In my early twenties I read the book *Prison to Praise* by Merlin Carothers. He helped me see that I could release any situation to God by praising Him. About ten years later, the story of Jehoshaphat in II Chronicles 20 became my favorite Bible story. Again, it was a story of releasing control. Jehoshaphat had three armies coming against him, and he had no hope of victory. The prophet told Jehoshaphat, **"the battle is not yours, but God's" (20:15).** The entire tribe of Judah marched out with the choir singing praises **"to see the salvation of the Lord."** It was an act of trust and obedience. I have given many situations to God, and I have learned how to release them in my spirit (not just my mind). Releasing the battle to God is the ultimate act of trust toward God. Through financial difficulties, breast cancer, miscarriage, and marital upsets—release has always been the best course available. Students have crises too. Families and friendships break-up. They need real answers to tough situations. True release is powerful. Here are the steps to giving God the battle.

- Relax and focus on Jesus inside you.

- Release the situation to God. Sometimes I ask Jesus to come in and through me and take the situation, evil thoughts, negative words, etc. from me.

- I thank God for taking the situation from me. This is the step that I repeat if the situation returns in my mind or life. This is the trust step. If I release it to Him, my goal is to leave it with Him.

The basic operation of releasing to God can also be used to give good things to God and others. When we worship from our spirit, we offer true worship (see John 4:23). I heard from one of my 1st grade student's parents that they found him worshipping by himself in his bedroom. I have seen at least three of my students this year worshipping in a deep way with our Bible songs. You can tell they are connecting with God in their spirits and releasing worship to Him.

Basic Operation: Forgive

Kirk was easily offended by the other children. He often would pout and respond angrily to other students. In chapel one day, he was noticeably angry. I sat down next to him and he pointedly laid out all of Bill's offenses. I reminded him of how Jesus was the perfect forgiver and that he could ask Jesus to forgive Bill for hurting him. Then Jesus would take his pain away too. It took Kirk several minutes to relax and realize he was the one paying for his anger. Once he yielded to Jesus and asked Him to forgive Bill, he was like a changed person. He was smiling and able to participate again in chapel. He had learned how to do this in Bible class, he just needed to be reminded.

The basic operation of forgiveness can be a daily exercise taught to children. The students do not have to even reveal who they are forgiving, they just need to be able to identify someone in their mind.

EXERCISE: Asking for Jesus to help us forgive someone who has hurt us.

1. Relax, close your eyes, and "open the door" of your innermost being or belly.

2. Ask the Holy Spirit to bring someone to mind that you need to forgive. Remember the feelings that come up when you remember this person. (You can ask your students to nod their heads when they have someone in mind, so they do not have to share out loud).

3. Ask Jesus, the perfect forgiver, to forgive that person and take away the pain. You can say something like, "Jesus, You are the perfect forgiver, please go in us and through us and forgive that person and take our pain away."

4. Ask if the hurt changed to peace. Ask for testimonies if anyone wants to share.[7]

I have used this many times for conflict resolution in the classroom. Usually, one child comes with a complaint. If it isn't a safety matter or a serious incident, I lead the child through letting Jesus forgive the other person. Often the matter is resolved right then and there.

This can also be a personal growth time, getting rid of fear, anger, guilt, shame, pride–any negative emotion. Negative emotions are basically taking the enemy's side against God. We want to get rid of these and have the fruit of the Spirit instead. I even model this for my students when I get frustrated in the classroom. I say, "Wait a minute, Mrs. Rensink needs to get rid of some anger and allow Jesus the forgiver to forgive her for getting angry." I pause and go through the exercise either silently or out loud (without naming anyone) and regain my peace. I am a much better teacher coming from peace. I have become much more sensitive to what is happening in my belly, so I can deal with it quickly. When I step out of peace into anger or fear, it is almost like an alarm goes off and I quickly use the basic operation of forgiveness to get rid of it.

Recording Progress

In kingdom education, we continually rebuild environments where students can connect to God. Students' ideas about prayer and connecting to God often hold them back. Because intimate prayer is seen as such a personal thing, it is difficult to model in a corporate setting. However, there are ways we can incorporate experiences which help make their relationship with God more personal.

A Jesus Journey Journal

Provide regular opportunities for students to make entries in their journal. Make it personal with pictures and the student's work. Hopefully it will be a keepsake they will refer to or use to build their own personal journal experience.

- Draw a picture of you doing something you would do with Jesus.

- Document times when you were sensitive to the Holy Spirit.

- Use an uplifting worship song and have the students draw a picture with three colors and strokes and circles while the music is playing.[8]

- Set aside some pages for "things I am thankful for" or "what God did for me."

- Build identity with Scripture pages on who we are in Christ. Discuss them with a partner and enter what that Scripture means to you.

Practice Make Perfect

The old saying that "practice makes perfect" can definitely be applied to spiritual intelligence operations. Giving students opportunities to experience Christ within and His enabling grace requires planning. It is not a one-time experience. Just like "faith *comes* by hearing" it is a repeated exercise that makes it real and allows growth. These operations, however, cannot become a ritual—they must be a personal inner encounter with Christ within. He is our all and He is in all! (see Colossians 3:11).

Endnotes

1. Gerhard Kittel, Editor. Theological Dictionary of the New Testament, Vol. 3, (Wm. B. Eerdmans Publishing Company, 1965) p. 613.

2. Alan Richardson, Editor. A Theological Word Book of the Bible, (MacMillan Publishing Company, 1950) p. 145.

3. Dennis and Dr. Jen Clark. Five Functions of the Human Spirit, (Full Stature Ministry, 2013) pp. 45-49.

4. Graham Cooke (Indwelling Presence, Disc 2, track 7)

5. Sarah Young, *Jesus Calling*, (Thomas Nelson, 2008) March 28

6. Kat Kerr, *Revealing Heaven II: An Eyewitness Account* (Xulon Press, 2010) pp. 132-4.

7. Dennis and Jen Clark, *The Great God Quest Series: Gold Goes to the School of the Spirit*, (2012) p. 43.

8. We use Scripture worship songs from Seeds Family Worship.

CHAPTER 13

FUN IS FUNDAMENTAL TO TEACHING: HOW ONE SOCIAL STUDIES TEACHER ENGAGES STUDENTS

by Clint Rogers

Introduction

I have been a teacher for over twenty years—inner city, suburban, rural, public and private schools—I've taught them all. In every environment I have taught in, there are some truths that exist across all spectrums. Gaining the interest of a teenager is hard. They are bored almost all of the time. If you can catch their interest, which is a feat in and of itself, their learning experience and your teaching experience will be vastly improved. How do you gain the interest of a teenager? By being unpredictable, a little crazy, but mostly it's applying the basic fundamental ideas of creating a "fun" classroom. Because let's face it, I get bored too. If I teach the same thing over and over, year after year, my creativity is going to die. You fight the boredom—theirs and yours—by creating a fun classroom. "Fun" does not mean there is no content, in fact this could not be further from the truth. If you are able to take your classroom and add a fun activity or practice to the content you are working on, the lessons will stick with the students, and you will be more likely to enjoy your time as well. "Fun" also does not mean "easy"—it takes effort to find the fun in what you are teaching. Fun is a key component of classes at CSCL and *fun* has kept me teaching with creativity and energy for over twenty years.

As a side note, while this chapter is centered on the subject of social studies, these principles can be applied to any subject. I include general concepts on issues concerning classroom teaching as well as more specific information about teacher operations in the subject area of social studies.

I have an outline at the end of this chapter for an approximate semester course of a typical United States history class. The outline includes the typical topics I have included in a normal survey of this course. I have also included some suggested creative and fun activities that you may consider when building your own course. Even if you do not teach a U.S. history course, this outline may inspire ideas geared towards your particular subject.

Mission and Concept (and fun!)

Missions. The *primary* mission of academic high school teachers is to prepare students in the various required academic disciplines required by the state they reside in. The primary mission of social studies teachers is to prepare students in the subject of the social sciences in order that they satisfy the diploma requirement of the subject in the state that they reside in. The standards and requirements vary from subject to subject and from state to state, but in the subject of social studies they tend to remain quite consistent among all of the fifty U.S. states. The *secondary* and perhaps more important mission(s) of the social studies' teacher are to develop, organize, equip, train, and direct students in the conduct of knowledge of social studies subjects such as citizenship, basic finances, and knowledge of past historical events. The other subject disciplines have individual specific target topics. After understanding the overarching goals of the course the teachers will be instructing, they can next begin at looking for how to work fun into these assigned topics and subjects.

Concept. In the same way that certain subject departments will be called upon to facilitate certain activities related to their subjects, Social studies' teachers may be called on to be responsible for the conduct of conventional or unconventional "social studies" activities within schools and may be called upon to perform other tasks associated with or in support of an administrators' suggestions. For social studies'. teachers, examples may include facilitating school elections, organizing student and school wide debates, gathering facts on possible field trips to local destinations or foreign lands, organizing cultural celebration days, and facilitating celebrations for a historical person or cultural highlight. These types of assignments are usually interesting, simply because they are not the same old same old routine.

Introducing Fun

The element of fun is an important part of any subject area classroom. All activities conducted in classes should, whenever possible, be tied into something that is considered fun and interesting, for the students and for the teacher as well. The field of social science has the primary component across all disciplines of *people*. This includes the study of people before recorded history, analysis of recorded historical events of certain people, and present-day ways of thinking, socializing, and the governing of one another as people. Generally, people and events that were interesting are more appealing to study and learn from than those people or events that were not. When operating a social studies' class, there is no reason that teachers cannot make lessons, discussions, and learning fun. The social studies' subject matter inherently covers topics such as conflict, war, romance, ancestry, dancing, food, inventions, and exploration among many others. When covering these topics, the social studies' teacher needs to constantly try and incorporate food, costumes, dramas and skits, music and dance, movies, debates, re-enactments, and primary source investigations.

Primary sources include actual historical objects that were used in the time period one is studying. These might include letters, weapons, maps, documents, audio and video recordings, and other items that were actually in the particular time period to be studied. Secondary sources are useful as well and these include books, interviews, accounts, and writings of others who were not present but are experts on the particular area of study. The most common examples of a secondary sources are textbooks. Teachers have to struggle to not rely too much on secondary sources such as textbooks. It might take more planning to find primary accounts, autobiographies, and interviews, etc., but it pays off in keeping a class more interesting and fun. Identifying each subject's discipline's theme can help the teacher and the students remember the subjects focus.

Teachers should be open to focusing on subjects and lessons that they themselves find interesting and exciting. By doing this, the students will detect more interest in those lessons themselves. There seems to be some kind of phenomena where students catch the motivation aspect of teachers that are motivated themselves. Too many schools and classrooms today are ruled by performance and scoring to the detriment of fun, what's interesting, and what one student might find some connection with in a subject of the past. When teachers show exuberance towards what is being studied and discussed, there is a marked difference in a class where the teacher obviously has little desire to cover or discuss the subject matter. All subject area teachers must strive to discover this in their own way to keep themselves and their students motivated. One of my most demanding and creative ideas was implemented in the summer of 2017. I got the idea that I would dress up as each of the forty-five American Presidents and involve my class in the project, however long it took. The idea was that I would grow out my hair and beard to the longest length needed for the "shaggiest" President (Rutherford Hayes) and then cut and shave my actual hair down to the most bald/hairless of the Presidents (Dwight Eisenhower) over the course of several weeks, taking a picture at each stage. I started growing my hair in the summer, and I was ready for the first picture at the beginning of the school year in the fall. I documented the whole experience and made it into a YouTube video and Instagram page—you can check it out at by looking up "Presidential Hair Challenge." I was quite proud of it. But perhaps the best part of the experience was when I walked into the classroom with my long beard and hair and told the class my idea. I opened up my first class by saying, "This is what I did this summer, what did you do?" And I challenged them to think about what kind of grand idea or scheme they could you come up with like this. This type of creative endeavor gives your student food for thought and perhaps inspires them to likewise do the same.

If you consider your own passions and what you might be interested in teaching, it will naturally make your students more interested. A highlighted example of this in U.S. history class would be teaching a history lesson on the 1970s in the United

States. If a teacher drones on about the rise of inflation, Arab embargoes, and the energy crisis solely by reading from the textbook, it can be challenging to peek the students' interest. But if the teacher takes some time before teaching that lesson to clear the desks and chairs from the classroom, and then shows the class how to dance the disco era dance steps of the Hustle, with the help of a YouTube instruction video, and then perhaps shows the opening scene to *Saturday Night Fever*, or an episode of *Real People* or *Battle of the Network Stars*, the teacher may find a more relaxed, receptive, and motivated student audience. The teacher may then begin discussing the 1970s and might also find a more interested classroom. Another technique I have used in my own classrooms is that I have identified specific places within certain films that cover historical topics that I need to cover in lecture. I will introduce the topic, teach about it, and then pause and show the part of the movie and that particular topic. We can then have a discussion, watch more of the film, or return to the lecture topics.

With the primary mission of social studies, or any subject area curriculum, being to prepare the students for recognized credits in order to receive approved credits for a state high school diploma, teachers do have to be aware of the content areas they are tasked to cover. While teachers should not feel overly restricted by standards or inhibited by "what I have to cover before the end of the course," there should be balance and a consideration of respect for the course guidelines to the extent that all, or the bulk of, the state/district standards are addressed during the course. Teachers should not completely leave recommended topics and teach 100% of their own chosen lessons. A student coming in or out of the class and going to a different school in the area should not be severely behind other students in similar classes. It is not difficult, however, to boil down critical topic areas and cover them while still weaving in fun lessons and experiences that the teachers themselves truly enjoy.

In any course area of content to teach, there is overlap that exists. The teacher should seek to creatively do this, which can free up time to allow for moments of fun in its place. In a typical American government course, there will be a designated unit on "comparative systems." This unit usually differentiates other countries' governments and how they are similar to the U.S. Republic government. Instead of spending a week on extensive details of governments in Japan or the United Kingdom, the teacher can highlight many differences between our system and other sovereign nations as they arise in the news of the day. The teacher can fulfill the compare and contrast aspect as they go through other sections. Once during a semester of an economics course, I brought one of my classes to a branch of the Federal Reserve Bank of Charlotte, N.C. During the tour, the guide reported that soon the use of personal checks would greatly diminish as well as other aspects of banking and monetary policy that the course guides still include in its set of objectives. We took that opportunity to compare and contrast the present use of cards and even digital pay options that we saw that day as we finished our tour, keeping an eye out if we saw anyone using a checkbook (they didn't). But the students were engaged in the conversation as we studied how personal banking has changed over time, and we speculated how it might change in the future.

The challenge to any teacher is to go boldly into the planning and implementation of the content and streamline where one can. The teacher should try and not dwell on what they may or may not be doing or missing if it saps their own joy and creativity in the classroom.

Special Equipment

In addition to the equipment necessary for the conduct of the typical course, such as textbooks, maps, and models, teachers may consider the following special equipment for use in the classroom in conducting successful, fun lessons. Record players, record albums, classic movies, VCRs (older devices such as reel to reel players, cassette and laser disc players), out of date textbooks, old maps, globes, old letters, newspapers, financial documents such as ledger books, checks, and old currency might be used. Period accounts of historical events such as audio, television interviews, plays, and diaries help to convey emotion and feelings of the people of those time periods.

A couple of success stories to illustrate these suggestions were Sarah and Margie. Both students were aloof during the normal class operations. Although one of the students was talkative and the other very quiet and reserved, both were not very engaged in my attempts to hold interactive discussion and debates. In both cases, when I introduced my extensive record album collection to the class, an interesting change occurred. While covering the decades of the 1920-80s, I often show my classes records from those decades. Sometimes I show them dance steps from the songs or maybe iconic movie clips that correspond to what was happening during those eras. Both Sarah and Margie seemed to completely switch gears and participate more going forward. They would ask to borrow the records and even bring in records of their own to show me. One student later gave me more records as a thoughtful gift, which I enjoyed. One of the students, even years later, will occasionally say hello and check in. Using additional fun props and resources might reach students where other means do not. Also, any kind of dancing in class is recommended. It takes a little "arm twisting" to get going, especially from the males, but almost every single time that I have taught various dances, every single student usually has a great time or at least smiles a wee bit. If you are teaching American history, there is the Charleston, East and West Coast Swing, the Jive, Lindy hop, 50's Rock 'n Roll Swing, the Mashed Potato, the Twist, the Watusi, etc. Also, there is obviously disco, break dancing from the 80s, hip-hop, and country line dancing as well—anything goes, and you may be surprised which students respond positively to this type of interaction and what they remember at the end of the course.

Do not forget to use living persons as experts and class speakers to enhance your classroom teaching. Military veterans, long-time local residents, young people participants, and other live storytellers can take the lesson to an entirely new level. Recently, a former Army Ranger spoke to my class about his experience as a Tomb of the Unknown Soldier guard. The talk quickly expanded and broadened and he ended up returning on many other occasions much to the delight of the students. He was warmly received by the entire class.

Teaching the Course

The course should be considered as having three primary parts: introduction, bulk of the course, wrap-up. This applies to any content subject area.

Introduction. The beginning of the social studies course or any subject course, should include three main parts. First, the teacher should solicit a thorough "student information" sheet that gathers background information on the students in the class. The purpose of this is to learn students' interests, what they consider fun, as well as locating places where students were born or lived. This information can be used later in class lessons when studying locations where these students have connections.

Second, the teacher should determine where the students are in terms of knowledge-base in the class to be taught. The best way to do this is to give a pre-test of topics that the course will seek to cover. If the teacher determines that most or all of the class have mastered a particular topic area, then that will open up more time for the teacher to employ creative, fun activities to enhance those even further. Lastly, the introductory wave period is where the teacher quickly establishes expectations and makes plain his or her philosophy and classroom procedures. Teachers should take as much time as possible connecting with the class, getting to know them, building relationships, facilitating interesting discussions, allowing outspoken students to speak, as well as seeking to make them laugh and enjoy the class. When teachers do this early on, more content and ground can be covered as the course proceeds because the students feel more comfortable as participants.

Bulk of the Course. The bulk of any particular course is the period after the introductory period, when teacher and students feel comfortable being creative, taking risks, and speaking their mind on controversial topics. The teacher may have to take more or less time and adjust according to the students of that particular class. At this point in the course, the teacher should largely know who likes to speak, who has to be urged to participate, potential discipline problems, which students have strong views, and largely what those are and where/how they have been formulated. By doing this as early as possible, the teacher is able to manage the class and facilitate certain lesson topics as they arise. Ideally, the teacher can call on students that have experience related to different topics. Also, if the teacher feels called to challenge a student or group of students on a particular topic or point, this can be done in a professional, respectful manner. This part of the course should correspond with whatever content area course guides the teacher can find for their particular course subject. These are readily available today on the Internet. A new teacher should start with the state they reside in and research the state's educational department resources. Most of the course guides for social studies' classes vary little from state to state. Many of the other core subject areas also share similar pacing and course guides. It is recommended that teachers be very familiar with their district and state standards to be in compliance as much as can be maintained. This goes for private or homeschool classes as well. If teachers at least refer to local course guides as references for their courses, they will feel confident that students in and around their locales are on similar pages in terms of core area content.

Wrap-up. The final section of the course is the conclusion of the teaching component of the course and the final evaluation of student progress from the course. A prevailing issue is the amount of content teachers are "supposed to cover" in a given period of time with the students. One of the most difficult parts of teaching certain social studies courses, such as the history sections, is that the content seems to be entirely too vast and seemingly impossible to cover completely and adequately. This is also very much the case in math courses and science courses such as chemistry and biology. The teacher needs to face this dilemma with focus and concentration. A teacher may wrestle a constant see-saw of doubt about spending too much time on a particular section and not adequately introducing other areas of the course. In the subject of social studies, a new teacher will sooner or later realize that it is just not possible to cover an entire course of all of U.S. history not to mention European or world history content in the time given to do it. The teacher has to, in a professional manner, decide how to best cover essential content, and leave behind certain topics that time simply will not allow to adequately cover. If a teacher attempts to cover all of this content, they run the risk of skimming over and speeding through the topics they teach so fast that very little may be actually retained by the students. This is just an inherent problem to teaching certain social studies courses.

The main idea is to strive to include the topics that you, the teacher, are passionate about and will provide fun and interesting learning experiences for the class. At the same time, teachers must be aware not to drift too far off from required state course content topics. The final examination should cover the mid or full term in various ways and the students need to be aware of this far in advance so they can prepare, if they choose to do so. Depending on the school or administrative leadership, some teachers might be able to substitute or reduce typical lengthy written exams with more subjective demonstrations of student work such as presentations, research papers, original films, art exhibits, etc., or some combination thereof of any of these sometimes known as portfolios. It's important to note that the teacher needs to be very clear of expectations and specific task guidelines so the student is aware of them with plenty of time to create accordingly.

The Conclusion Plus a Few More Daring Ideas

The primary objective for any teacher in a K-12 setting is to make sure students that have taken the class are satisfactorily prepared in the particular required course they are assigned. For social studies teachers, U.S. history, economics and government, and world studies are the required courses for each state's diploma requirement. Other core subject departments have similar two, three, or four course requirements. The teacher must ascertain the best way to satisfactorily do this in the department they are a part of by researching the state's educational resources in these matters. Each teacher should also meet with and question their principal, admin, and department colleagues to determine their individual attention to these matters as well.

The secondary mission(s) of any K-12 teacher is to introduce, expose, develop, organize, equip, train, and direct students to the content areas as much as time will allow. In social studies, major examples are citizenship, basic finance, and knowledge of past historical events. Teachers should use a variety of activities that contain these types of concepts. The more interesting and fun these activities are for the student, the more the teacher will feel pride and accomplishment as a teacher. Also, if the teacher himself is actually enjoying these activities students see this and it seems to motivate them to engage and participate more. Frequent class discussions, dialogues, and Socratic question sessions are easy and great place to start when starting out. These can be used in other subjects such as math and science. For example, a lengthy discussion of the reasons why important math thinkers such as Descartes or Aristotle experimented with the concepts they did can be very interesting discussion. In any group setting, there seems to always be people that like to talk and share ideas. In social studies, students should engage in class debates, recite historical writings, and plan and make class speeches.

Even more daring ideas are assigning students to make simple films and/or projects to present to their class and school and even communities. Students can also teach lower grade classes on topics they are learning. Other common fun suggestions for any course subject would be field trips, going to movies, community visits to local important persons, local museums, and historical sites. All of these ideas can be applied to any course. When teaching a government course during local and national elections, students should be taken out to participate in campaigning and voting when possible. In areas of economics and finance, students can work on future budgets or plan a hypothetical future wedding in groups. Teachers may identify local charity events and have students participate as a class. Teachers may also have students open bank accounts, or play stock market and Forex simulations.

Another idea I strongly recommend is to play as much music as you can in your classes and then create a "soundtrack." Make a CD or digital file of songs that the students will always connect with the class and give each student a copy. For example, in a U.S. history class, going through the period before the Civil War and beyond, a teacher could present the songs *James K. Polk (They Might Be Giants*, a favorite of mine), *Bonnie Blue Flag, Dixie,* or James Brown's *Body.*

These examples are wonderful learning opportunities that students will relish when added to routine lectures and book assignments. Each course and each subject department have inherent fun aspects that go along with the subject. The difficulty of deploying these activities is they take time, planning, and risk-taking on the part of the teacher. Another suggestion that can help is for teachers to reflect on their own memories of fun learning experiences from when they were younger students themselves. Recall an unforgettable fun class activity and use it once again. It was memorable for some reason!

It is important to note that teachers should seek to associate with other creative teachers in a school setting when trying to create fun class experiences. They will inspire, encourage, and even challenge one another. Teachers should be aware that hanging around cynical and burnt out personnel may rub off on them. If the reader is doubtful of this, try the following experiment. Approach one of the latter type staff mentioned above and tell them of a very risky, wild idea for a class lesson and then observe the feedback that they may receive. Sadly, it's not difficult for a hardened cynic to extinguish the optimism of a risk-taking teacher.

Fun is not easy. But it's an important part of the classroom. If nothing else, my classes will always be fun and interesting. When I started teaching, I taught the standard 50-minute classes. Now at CSCL, some of my classes are 150 minutes in length. We are talking two and a half hour classes with 8th graders, people! Having a fun classroom is practically a necessity to survive such a scenario. I have students come back to see me after they have graduated, and without fail they bring up some crazy thing we did in a class—some dance or battle reenactment. It's a fun memory, but it also shows me the lessons that have stuck with them, even if the lesson was just "have fun and learn something new." So, take a risk and try something wild—grow out your hair or challenge the students to a dance-off. If you have fun, they will too. And they will never forget it.

If anyone would like any clarification or like to discuss other related topics, feel free to contact me at csclrogers@gmail.com.

Appendix - Fun Ideas for All Major U.S. History Course Topics

Listed below is a sample course guides for the study of United States history. Included are the most common subject topics required of the course along with "creative/fun" activities for teachers to consider when building their own courses. Although this guide is specific to history, teachers of other disciplines may think of uses suited for their area after reading below.

United States History

Fundamental historical knowledge of:

- **Events leading to the settlement of the British American colonies**
  Map games, puzzles, geography of Americas and European colonizers, plays, skits, films covering Native American stories and Puritan life, mock witch trial

- **The colonial period including the Revolutionary War**
  Films: Last of the Mohicans, The Patriot, 1776; act out 1776 musical play, memorize/recite portions of Declaration of Independence

- **The establishment of the U.S. Constitution, 1787-1797**
  Documentaries: Writing the Constitution, Hamilton, John Adams HBO series

- **Period of Political Parties, 1797-1820**
  Read and discuss Federalist Papers, memorize and recite sections of Federalist papers, read political attack ads/ commentary of times of Adams and Jefferson and compare to more modern campaigns of Obama and Trump, documentary: Burn's Lewis and Clark, research Cajun Acadians settlement of Louisiana and the cook Cajun creole recipes with zydeco music

- **Early American History before 1861**
  Study and act out life of Andrew Jackson, Trail of Tears study and create story tales, hold mock debates between south and north over popular sovereignty and states' rights, study Supreme Court case Drew Scott, read Uncle Tom's Cabin, Documentary: John Brown, learn and play John Brown's Body song, Dixie song

- **The American Civil War and Reconstruction**
  Documentary: Burn's The Civil War, play Civil War battle simulator games, visit era battlegrounds and sites, dress and act out period women and men's skits of the times, Films: Glory, Lincoln; read Red Badge of Courage, find local gunsmith to exhibit muzzle loader rifles, visit Civil War era re-enactments

- **The American Industrial Era including the Progressive Movement**
  Study biography of wealthy capitalists, compare/contrast study report of Carnegie, Rockefeller to Gates, Jobs, Zuckerberg; dress up mystery murder suspect play Theodore Roosevelt, visit Biltmore House, read Upton Sinclair's, The Jungle

- **American Imperialism era including WW1, WW2, Korean and Vietnamese Conflicts, Involvement in Iraq**
  Films/documentaries of World War 1,2; interview veterans of military service, Films: Forest Gump, Saving Private Ryan, study rise of Korean/Vietnamese nationalism, watch CNN broadcasts of Gulf and Iraq conflicts

- **Liberal and Conservative politics from 1960 to the present**
  Study writings/interviews: Barry Goldwater, Phyllis Schafly, Abbie Hoffman, Martin Luther King Jr., John and Robert Kennedy, Richard Nixon, Jimmy Carter, Ronald Reagan; Listen to speeches, interview Family members about this era, learn dance moves/music of 50s, 60s, 70s; skits of beatniks, hippies, protesters

OUTDOOR LEADERSHIP

by Al Franklin

Origins:

Outdoor Leadership began as an elective course to develop students' appreciation of nature and the Creator. The elective honors Jon Amos Comenius, who believed education stems from interaction with God's natural world.

Long-Term Goals:

Students stretch mentally, physically, and spiritually through interaction with nature. They master basic survival skills and learn to lead a group. The outdoor activities are also intended to cultivate a greater awareness of God's messages within nature.

Spiritual, Creative, and Leadership Activation

Spiritual:

- Students learn to hear God's voice in any environment.

- Students develop skills in creating and delivering devotional messages.

Creative:

- Students handle available resources and "make do" when they are scarce.

- Students develop practical ways to serve their community.

Leadership:

- Students develop awareness of themselves—how well they lead, their strengths and weaknesses, and their level of responsibility within a group.

- Students learn self-reliance and focus when physically and mentally tested.

- Students learn basic teamwork skills, including cooperation and appreciation for others' strengths.

Academic Objectives:

Students develop basic skills in orienteering, camping, water navigation, identifying local plants, and problem-solving techniques.

Suggested Materials:

Students need access to essential hiking and camping equipment (see Appendix). The school supplies all food and cooking utensils for the camping trips. Students also need bicycles and bicycle helmets.

Each student pays a $100-$150 cover charge, due the first day of class. This cover charge pays for campsites and provisions, canoe/kayaking rentals, and camping gear rental, if applicable.

Semester Plan:

Outdoor Leadership is a seven-week elective course. Class meets all-day Monday through Thursday. The following sample schedule reflects a typical Outdoor Leadership semester. This course schedule is adaptable to your own school schedule, resources, and availability of off-site activities.

Class size should not exceed twenty students. Larger classes require additional instructors to ensure student safety.

Volunteers or interns help administrate class activities. High-School interns (see Appendix) typically have a similar class schedule as middle school students, making them readily available. Interns focus on developing leadership skills during their internship.

Week 1	Monday	Devotion: Teacher-Led Intro to Class - Expectations and Safety PE - stretching and warm ups Teamwork exercise Compass Lab Begin Treasure Map
	Tuesday	Devotion-Student 1 PE Hiking: local location (take notes on plant life and animals) Lunch in the woods Treasure Map Planning Time
	Wednesday	Devotion: Student 2 PE Quiz on Hiking Trail notes Team Building Game Reading Time: camping gear and do's and don'ts Treasure Hunt Planning time for Community Project
	Thursday	Devotion: Student 3 PE Team building game: Ultimate Frisbee Wash camping gear in preparation for trip Plan for next week's Bike Hike and camping

Week 2	Monday	Devotion: Student 4 PE Bike check (tire pressure) Bike Hike to local greenway location Lunch at location Bike back
	Tuesday	Devotion: Student 5 PE Prepare for Campout Head to Camp destination - spend the night Team building games at location Make Camp (if weather is severe, camp at school)
	Wednesday	Devotion: Student 6 PE at location after breakfast Team exercise/mental challenge Reading time: local information Break Camp
	Thursday	Devotion: Student 7 PE Quiz on Camping Notes Overview of Rope-tying Planning for Community Project
Week 3	Monday	Devotion: Student 8 PE Begin Community Project
	Tuesday	Devotion: Student 9 PE Complete Community Project
	Wednesday	Devotion: Student 10 PE Teach basic canoe strokes and canoe parts Reading Time: about canoe location Review of knot lessons, demonstrations
	Thursday	Head to Canoe Destination Devotion at canoe location: Student 1 Canoe and hike

Week 4	Monday	Devotion: Student 2 PE Quiz on Canoe strokes and location Teamwork Game Reading Time Build Water Bottle Rockets
	Tuesday	Devotion: Student 3 PE Knot Tying Application (rescue and camping) "River Rescue" challenge, using knot-tying skills to cross a "river" Plan Bike Hike
	Wednesday	Devotion: Student 4 Pack bikes in trailer and head to different location Warm Ups Bike Hike greenway trails
	Thursday	Devotion: Student 5 PE Basketball/Tennis exercises Begin Research projects
Week 5	Monday	Devotion: Student 6 PE Team building exercise Students teach knot-tying to younger grade
	Tuesday	Devotion: Student 7 PE Quiz on Bike Trail notes Team Exercise Reading Time: sailboat overview
	Wednesday	Devotion: Student 8 Travel to destination for kayaking
	Thursday	Devotion: Student 9 Travel to sailboat location Sailboat safety overview Sail boating and swimming

Week 6	Monday	Devotion: Student 10 PE Fishing Trip (catch and release)
	Tuesday	Devotion: Student's Choice PE Computer lab - research papers/presentations Plan final Camping Trip
	Wednesday	Devotion: Student's Choice PE Whitewater center activities
	Thursday	Devotion: Student's Choice Students give presentations, turn in reports Devotion logs due
Week 7	Monday	Devotion: Student's Choice Finish student presentations Reading Time/plan for Camping Trip Clean camping gear/prep
	Tuesday	Travel to Camping location Intro to State Park by Park Rangers Q&A with Park Rangers Overview of safety precautions - discuss emergency plans Set up camp Explore/Hike (devotional time) Students build campfire and cook evening meal Nighttime: star gazing and satellite view
	Wednesday	Breakfast/Devotional Hiking/exploring Group activities Night Time: school year reflections, encouraging words
	Thursday	Breakfast/ Final Devotion Clean campsite Break camp

Daily Class Structure

Each class day begins with the following:

- Physical Education (PE): Includes a warm up, basic PE activities, and stretching (see Appendix). PE conditions students for the physical demands of the course. The goal is to improve flexibility, endurance, and coordination.

- Devotions: Students take turns preparing and presenting devotions. The goal is to develop skills in articulating spiritual beliefs and leading a group. Students not presenting will take notes on major insights learned from the devotion.

- Class Activity: Each class is centered on a major activity. Students read about the activity (or destination) before completing the event. Reading time provides a context for the destination or activity.

- End of Class: Class ends with a summation of major information or with a weekly quiz.

Major Activities Overview

Students engage in a variety of outdoor activities that build on each other over a seven week period. Each activity includes an outing or team-building exercise that reinforces a lesson. These lessons culminate in the final week of class. The activities listed are in the order they are typically covered.

- Compass Lab: Students learn to read a compass and perform basic orienteering. This lab occurs during the first week of the class. Camping and hiking trips are based on this introduction to orienteering.

- Local Hiking/Biking: Students explore areas beyond the school building. During excursions, they identify safe and unsafe plants.

- Team Building Games: Students develop skills in leading and following. The exercises also encourage discovery of strengths and weaknesses. Team members learn to rely on each other to complete a task.

- Constructing a Wooden Seat: Students build a wooden seat of their own design. Each person contributes to the construction. The goal is to become familiar with basic tools, such as hammers, saws, and levels. Students also practice teamwork.

- Community Project: The class works together to improve the school or local community. Two class days are generally devoted to the service project.

- Major Outdoor Activity: Students complete an outdoor activity requiring mastery of a new skill. Determine available activities that take at least a full day to complete. Sail boating, snow skiing, and archery are examples of appropriate skill building activities. Students should receive instruction on how to perform the activity prior to the event.

- Other Activities: Take students into nature often. Focus on basic survival skills and teach them to notice details. Activities also include a lake or river excursion to introduce canoeing/kayaking.

- Research and Presentation Project: Students study the life of a famous explorer and their contribution to our understanding of the natural world. The information is presented to the class during week 6. This is the last major graded assignment.

- Final Camping Trip: Students camp in the wild for at least two nights during the final week of class. This is the culminating event of the course. The camping trip is not a graded assignment; students simply exhibit mastery of skills learned throughout the course. Any student may be chosen to demonstrate a task.

Major Activities Guidelines

Compass Lab - Week 1:

Begin with an overview of compass points and basic orienteering. Acquaint students with using a compass, reading a map, and marking paces.

Create a Map:

Students make a map of the school building and surrounding area using graph paper. They layout major rooms/buildings, measure paces, and note significant landmarks.

Design a Treasure Map:

Separate the class into two teams. Each team creates a "treasure map" directing the other team to a specific location. The treasure map is based on the graph paper sketch. A "treasure" of the teacher's choosing is hidden (our students enjoy having cupcakes as the reward). The teams exchange maps and race to find the hidden treasure. The winning team receives the reward.

Designing the map takes half a class day. Locating the treasure takes approximately a quarter of class time.

Grading the Activity:

Each student is graded on their individual maps and orienteering skill demonstrated during the treasure hunt. The team is graded on the reliability of their treasure map. Points are deducted if the map is inaccurate or the directions misleading. The team also loses points if they fail to follow the other team's map.

The winning team receives a bonus grade. Quizzes for this lab are based off of the students' notes.

Local Hiking/Biking:

The class explores an area within walking or biking distance of the school. If the school is in an urban environment, transport the students (and bikes) to a safe location, such as a local greenway or park. The area should contain a wide variety of plant life. Familiarize yourself with local plant and animal life prior to the outing.

Hiking and biking can be done in any weather with proper safety precautions. Train students in bike safety, including how to wear a helmet, check tire pressure, and use hand signals on streets and highways. Typical hiking/biking trips are 3-5 miles in duration.

Students experience two hikes during the seven week course; one four mile hike and a three to four mile one during the final camping trip. Biking trips also occur at least twice.

Students carry notebooks or clipboards during hiking/biking trips. Identify a plant or animal while the students take notes. These notes culminate into a quiz at the end of the week.

The content of the quizzes differ every semester based on what the class encounters that year.

Team Building Games

Teaching students to work within a team is essential to developing capable leaders. This course fosters this skill through a variety of team building games. Demanding team exercises encourages students to rely on each other to accomplish a task.

Design unique team building exercises or pull them from other sources. The Boy Scouts of America website is an excellent source for team-building games. The challenge and its setting should vary. Exercises should stretch students' problem-solving ability. The goal is to develop students' skills in leading and following. Students learn to value the strengths of their team members while acknowledging their own. Designate a new team leader for every game to ensure that each student experiences the leadership role.

Designed by Al Franklin, the following exercises have been used successfully as fun yet challenging activities to foster this type of team building experience.

Outdoor Leadership Team Building Game: Torch Race

Goal:

Students problem-solve to light a series of oil lamps using only a bundle of sticks, wicks, and string/rubber bands. This is a fun activity for the first campout.

Materials:

The race requires three oil lamps, a bundle of medium-sized sticks, a wick, and string or rubber bands per team.

Setup:

Divide students into two teams. Place each team's oil lamps in a clearing, beyond a starting line. The first oil lamp is placed several feet from the starting line. Each team receives a torch and then they march to the set up area.

Activity Directions:

Once reaching the location where the oil lamps have been planted, the teams determine how to light the first oil lamp without crossing over the starting line. Students must use the string/rubber bands, wicks, and sticks to accomplish the task. Problem-solving is needed to determine the best way to bind the sticks together. Once the sticks are assembled, the wick is tied at the end and lit. A team member is selected to light the first oil lamp. The team must work together to keep the lamp lighter from crossing over the line as they lean out to light the lamp.

Once the first oil lamp is lit, the team moves to that lamp and attempts to light the second one. Increase the distance between the second and third lamps so that each attempt to light the lamp is harder than the last. If it is windy, the team selects a person to protect the flame from being extinguished. If a lamp goes out, the team must start again from that lamp.

Teams should encourage each other during the activity. The first team to light all three oil lamps wins a prize of the teacher's choosing.

Follow-up:

Discuss the significance of the experience. Remind the students that they are all on the same camping trip and should encourage members of both teams, not just their own. Draw a parallel between brothers and sisters in Christ who come from different churches or countries. Discuss how we are engaged in similar tasks and difficulties even though we are lighting different 'candles.' Consider how only one torch was used to light each lamp, yet the light spread much further when lit by a team rather than an individual. Keeping truth in one place is easy, but spreading it takes teamwork.

Outdoor Leadership Team Building Game: Country Activity

Country Activity: Barter and Trade – Part 1

Goal:

Students exercise creativity in designing a country using available resources.

Materials:

Paper and/or poster board and colored pencils.

Setup:

Place students into groups of three. These groups are called "countries" for the remainder of the exercise.

Activity Directions:

Each country works as a team to create the following:

- Design and draw a map of their country using color pencils

- Name the country

- Label the capital, major cities, roads, and terrain features

- Design a flag, including the symbolic meaning of the design

- Create a history for the country, including major imports/exports, customs/traditions, and what the people of the country are known for.

Each country presents their information to the other countries.

Country Activity: Barter and Trade – Part 2

Goal:

Students adequately assess the needs of a group and the available resources to meet those needs.

Materials:

Prepare a resource bag for each country. The resource bag contains symbols of resources like timber, water, gems, and produce. Construct the symbols from colored scraps of paper or whatever material is available.

Supply each country with varying amounts of each resource and an information sheet detailing the country's needs. Resources are not equal to the countries' needs. One country will have a surplus of a resource while another will have a shortage. An excess of resources depicts major world countries while shortages symbolize struggling countries.

Activity Directions:

Each country is given a set amount of time to reach agreement about their needs. Countries barter and trade with each other to see if they can adequately provide for those needs.

Follow-up:

Discuss the world at large and consider countries that have enough vs. countries that do not have enough. Engage in intercession for America and other countries. Students should also express their observations about the exercise. Consider how each team functioned, the strengths and weaknesses that emerged, and so on.

Sample of Country Resources:

	Timber	Water	Silk	Diamonds	Fruit/Produce
Country 1 Has:	10	7	5	6	7
Country 1 Needs:	5	5	3	3	6
Country 2 Has:	4	1	3	3	6
Country 2 Needs:	5	3	2	2	4
Country 3 Has:	2	2	2	1	3
Country 3 Needs:	3	1	1	2	2
Country 4 Has:	2	5	0	0	6
Country 4 Needs:	4	3	1	2	5
Country 5 Has:	7	3	0	0	2
Country 5 Needs:	4	5	2	1	4
Country 6 Has:	0	5	0	0	1
Country 6 Needs:	4	3	1	0	4

Constructing a Wooden Seat

Goal:

Students' design and build a simple wooden seat that will hold up a student for at least sixty seconds. This project encourages their creativity in design, ability to improvise, and teamwork skills. Basic knowledge of hand tools and building mechanics is also developed.

Setup:

Divide the class into three or four groups. Give each group access to basic tools and wood. Scrap wood and 2x4s works best for this project. Students practice thinking outside of familiar designs when working only with the available resources.

Activity Directions:

Teams draw out their designs and receive feedback on the design's feasibility. Once designs are approved, teams construct their wooden seats. Each student participates in the seat's construction. Students waiting to make their contribution can practice using a hammer and nails, saw, or drill. This system provides everyone with the opportunity to master the basic function of each tool. Once the project is complete, teams select individuals to demonstrate their creation's ability to hold up a student for a period of time.

Follow-up:

Conduct a debrief session with the students. Discuss the design and construction process. Allow students to express any frustrations the team experienced and how they worked together to overcome those challenges. Point out the importance of the skills learned to their everyday lives.

Community Service Project

Goal:

This project raises students' awareness of the world outside the classroom. Students demonstrate practical ways to support their local community.

Setup:

Research needs in the local church, school, or neighborhood. The needs may be small and easily accomplished or demanding, requiring a greater time commitment. Many clean-up projects will require special permission from students' parents and the various locations prior to the event.

Examples of community projects include:

- Students clearing debris from a neighborhood lake and greenway

- Students removing broken playground equipment using simple machinery and tools

- Students washing, polishing, and painting the school's bus

Major Outdoor Activity:

Students learn a new skill through a team project. The goal is to teach students to contribute while also learning to depend on others' strengths in order to succeed. Be creative in developing this activity, but it should require team work and mastery of a new skill.

Example: A parent offered our school the use of his sailboat. The students learned to properly rig, steer, and sail the boat. The teacher delegated project assignments so that each student was responsible for contributing towards the class' common goal.

Other Activities

Nature Scavenger Hunt

Complete this activity during the first hike. Divide students into teams and provide them with a list of local flora and fauna to identify while on the hike. Supply each team with a nature guide to help them identify items on the list. The team who correctly identifies the most items on the list is awarded a prize of the teacher's choosing. See the Appendix for a sample scavenger hunt list.

Knot Tying

Students identify and tie basic knots. This skill helps them perform class activities like sailing, hiking, and camping. Demonstrate, practice, and use the knots the same day. Explain that knot tying is a basic life skill that students can use outside of the classroom. Mr. Franklin, the originator of the Outdoor Leadership course, demonstrates a bowline knot and a clove hitch and explains that he uses these knots to secure his family's luggage on vacation.

Canoe Strokes

It is essential to teach proper form and function of various canoe strokes before going canoeing; most students do not naturally know how to grip paddles or coordinate strokes. Have students kneel on desks or table tops gripping paddles and practicing their technique. Students rotate the front and rear positions to learn how to control and steer a canoe.

On the water, students continue to practice various canoe techniques. This culminates in a demonstration of different canoe strokes as part of their course grade.

Filtering/Purifying Drinking Water

Provide an overview of the dangers of drinking unfiltered water prior to the first major outing. Students learn how to purify water during the first camping trip. Excursions to local parks/greenways provide additional opportunities to practice water purification. Incorporate students' notes from the discussion into the weekly quiz.

Fishing

Students learn basic fishing skills at a local lake, stream, or catch-and-release site. The goal is for students to experience a means of acquiring food. This exercise is also useful for introducing students to various fish life in the area.

Building a Campfire

Students build a basic campfire using various methods. Fire-safety procedures and extinguishing a campfire before exiting an area is also demonstrated. This lesson is taught prior to the first overnight camping trip where students practice this new skill.

On subsequent overnight trips, place various students in charge of starting the campfire. Include information on fire building methods and safety in the weekly class quiz.

Spontaneous Devotions

Ask the students for impromptu devotions during hikes or camping trips. The students separate from each other while remaining in visual contact with the teacher. They observe nature and talk to God about what they are seeing with the expectation that He will speak to them. The teacher also presses into God at this time and demonstrates the ability to hear from God in a natural environment. After approximately twenty minutes, gather the group together. Each student shares what God showed them.

Graded Assignments

Quizzes

Weekly quizzes are based on students' notes taken while out hiking, biking, camping, or participating in other activities.

Nature Scavenger Hunt

The nature scavenger hunt is graded like a quiz. Four points are deducted for each item the team fails to locate or identifies incorrectly. Because this is a team activity, the entire team receives the same grade.

Canoe Skills

Students are assessed on their knowledge of canoe parts. Questions about various paddle strokes are also included in the assessment.

PE Grade

PE sessions occur daily throughout the course. Students are assessed on their level of cooperation and attitude/effort displayed.

Bible Grade

The Bible grade is comprised of students' participation in devotions and the completion of their devotion journal. Students earn credit for a thoughtfully prepared devotion and displaying an enthusiastic attitude while presenting. Submitting a completed devotion journal at the end of the course is also factored into the final Bible grade.

Explorer Research Report and Presentation

The explorer research report and presentation is the final graded assignment of this course. The goal is for students to encounter a range of explorers from various countries and time periods.

Students select an explorer from a class list and write a paper reporting on that individual's life and accomplishments. On the day their paper is due, each student gives an oral presentation on their explorer. The paper and presentation should cover the major routes traveled by the explorer, the explorer's major life experiences, and their contribution to mapping and/or understanding the world.

Additional assignment guidelines and grading rubric is up to the creativity of the teacher. This assignment is completed in week 6, before the final campout.

See the Appendix for a list of explorers.

Typical Grading Distribution

Scavenger Hunt	5%
Canoe Skills	5%
Quizzes	10%
PE Grade	10%
Bible Grade	20%
Research Presentation	20%
Research Report	30%

Devotion Guidelines

Present the first devotion as a model for how to prepare and lead devotions. On the first day of class, students sign up for a day to be a devotion leader. Students may be responsible for two or three devotions if there are additional class days.

The general devotion structure consists of the following:

- Reading a favorite bible verse or chapter

- Explaining what the verse means to the individual student

- Applying the verse to the student's life

- Demonstrating how the verse can be applied to the student's classmates

The class typically opens with devotions. On hiking or biking trips, students practice responsibility by being prepared to present their devotion in the wild.

Students not presenting keep a journal recording personal thoughts and insights from each of the daily devotions. This devotion journal is included in the students' class grade as a completion assignment. Students must record each day's devotion to receive credit.

Sample Research Project Assignment Sheet:

From the class list of famous historical explorers, select an explorer for your research project. You may also propose an explorer of your choosing and submit it for approval.

Research Report:

Research your explorer and write 3-4 typed pages (double-spaced) providing historical accounts of the explorer and the contribution(s) they have made to the knowledge of and understanding of the world. Notes and drafts will be checked periodically to follow your progress during the last few weeks of class.

Oral Presentation:

Be prepared to present your explorer to the class, explaining the major points you covered in your written report. You will need to prepare note cards to read from. Be prepared to answer questions about the explorer.

Visual Aide:

As part of your presentation, create a map that details the route(s) traveled by your explorer and the main discoveries for which they are known.

Computer Time:

You will have in-class time to work on your report, but you may also need to work on this from home. On rainy days when we can't go outside, be prepared to research and work on your report.

Final Camping Trip: Week 7 / Last week of the Course

The course culminates in an extended camping trip (at least two nights) after all major grades are submitted. This trip functions primarily as a final time of exploration and bonding. Students demonstrate what they have learned over the seven weeks of class. Skills to demonstrate include plants to avoid, how to purify water, how to build a campfire, and how to navigate using basic orienteering skills.

Provide the food along with the cooking and eating utensils. The students provide the remaining basic camping needs (see Appendix). Students set up camp, cook the food over the campfire, and clean up the campsite at the end of the trip.

Day One:

Introduce the area and provide a safety overview. If possible, meet with a park ranger and allow students to ask questions about safety and the local plant and animal life.

Day one activities include:

- Games

- Hiking and exploring

- Setting up camp and building the campfire

- Preparing food for the group

- Stargazing and satellite watch

- Campfire stories/songs

Conduct an astronomy satellite view on the first night if the sky is clear. Students lie on a tarp spread in a field while the teacher points out the constellations. Wait for a satellite to cross over the heavens. Compete to see who is the first to spot the satellite.

Day Two:

Spend the day exploring and experiencing nature. Provide opportunities for students to demonstrate the skills they have learned during the course.

Encourage students to find a safe yet special place to spend time with God. Students have been trained to present spontaneous devotions, and this is an opportunity to receive a message from the Holy Spirit to share with the group. Ask them to record in a notebook what He is speaking to them through the environment.

The last night of the camping trip is an important one. Set aside the final evening as a time of encouragement and exhortation. Gather the class around the campfire and share specific encouraging words with each other and then the class as a whole. Discuss how each student has grown over the last seven weeks. Close with your own encouraging words to the students. Finish the evening with hot chocolate and a snack.

Appendix

High School Interns:

The teacher and students benefit from including high school interns in the course. Interns are assistants to the teacher and mentors to the students. They also gain valuable leadership training, which is a major goal of the intern program. The interns are usually seniors, but mature juniors can be effective as well. At least one male and one female intern serve throughout the course.

As assistants, the interns take charge of some outdoor activities and help facilitate hiking trips. They support struggling students and solve minor problems that arise. Interns must be mature and spiritually capable of providing counsel and advice. This is invaluable in most classes; younger students are more comfortable talking about issues with other students than with parental figures or teachers.

As role models, interns share their knowledge of high school with the middle school students. Time is set aside during the seven weeks of class for a Q&A about high school classes, expectations, and graduation. The interns give advice about what classes students need to take to graduate and answer basic questions about school. If they have experience with online classes, the interns discuss how to take them, explaining the benefits and drawbacks they have experienced. If they are seniors, the interns talk about their plans after graduation and how it feels to be a senior.

Camping Equipment Guide

The following is a general list of recommended equipment for camping trips. The first campout is an introductory experience. Equipment like a burner and cooler are recommended. Access to restrooms and pure drinking water on this trip are also encouraged. The final campout is intended to be more rustic experience. Students carry everything by backpack, filter their own drinking water, cook over an open fire, and do not usually have access to good restrooms.

- Lightweight 4-man tents

- Sleeping bags

- Large tarp

- Rope

- Flashlights or headlamps

- Hatchet

- Fire starter
- Fire pit grate
- Cooking and eating utensils
  - Pots
  - Pans
  - Large Spoon
  - Forks
  - Cups
  - Spatula
  - Knife
- Brillo pad
- Soap
- Paper towels
- Baby wipes
- Oven mitts
- First aid kit
- Compass
- Non-perishable snack items
- Camp food
  - Mac-and-cheese
  - Oatmeal

- Ramen noodles

- Dry Packaged soap

- Dry packaged pasta meals

- Other non-perishable, quick cooking, and lightweight foods

Nature Scavenger Hunt

This is a sample list for the nature scavenger hunt activity. Create a list that will reflect your local flora and fauna. This activity occurs during the first campout.

- One flower from a tree or plant

- One leaf from a tulip poplar tree

- One small granite rock

- Compound leaflet from Virginia Creeper vine

- One small rock of quartz or quartzite

- A little bit of moss from tree base or the ground

- Any scat from a wild animal

- Scale-like leaves from an evergreen like a cedar

- Hickory tree leaf or leaflet

- A dead shed pine tree needle in its bundle (2 or 3 needles)

- Some crustose lichen on a dead twig

- Small dead pine cone

- One piece of a bracket fungus

- Some foliage lichen

- One small live toad

- One small fern frond

- One good sized tall grass blade (parallel veins)

- One three-leafed clover with a bloom

- One 'most ridiculous' item not expected to find here

- One most colorful item that you can find

List of Explorers

Leif Ericson – Norse explorer who is regarded as the first European to land in North America ahead of Columbus.

Ferdinand Magellan – Portuguese explorer who was the first to sail from the Atlantic Ocean into the Pacific Ocean.

Christopher Columbus – Italian explorer who completed four voyages across the Atlantic.

Bartholomew Diaz – Portuguese explorer who was the first to complete an expedition around the Cape of Good Hope.

Hernando de Soto – Spanish explorer who led the first European expedition deep into the Southeastern Mississippi River region.

James Cook – British explorer and astronomer who led expeditions to the Pacific Ocean, Alaska. and Antarctica.

Jean Ribault – French naval officer who navigated and colonized much of Florida and the Southeastern United States.

Jacques Cousteau – French naval officer, undersea explorer, scientist, innovator, photographer, and author.

Sir Francis Drake – English sea captain, privateer, and navigator who led a three year expedition around the world.

Francis Younghusband – British army officer, explorer, and spiritual writer who traveled to the far east.

Henry Hudson – English explorer and navigator who led expeditions around New York and Canada.

John Smith – English adventurer and soldier who helped establish the first permanent English settlement in America.

Jedediah Smith – Hunter, trapper, trailblazer and explorer of the Rocky Mountains.

Daniel Boone – Early American frontiersman who explored Kentucky and the Appalachian Mountains.

David Crockett – Frontiersman, hunter, and Congressman who was later involved in the Battle of the Alamo.

Robert Peary – American naval officer and explorer who led the first expedition to the North Pole.

Henry Flagler – American industrialist who developed the Florida East Coast Railway all the way to the Florida Keys.

Sylvia Earle – American oceanographer and adventurer who set records in deep diving.

Dawn Wright – Geologist who studies structures along mid-ocean ridges.

Amelia Earhart – Famous pilot and record setting adventurer.

Bessie Coleman – First African American woman to stage a public flight.

Steve Fossett – American businessman who was a record setting aviator, sailor, and adventurer.

Apollo Astronauts:

> **Buzz Aldrin**
>
> **Neil Armstrong**
>
> **Eugene Cernan**
>
> **Michael Collins**
>
> **Charles Conrad**
>
> **John Glenn**
>
> **James Lovell**
>
> **Frank Borman**
>
> **Richard Gerdau**

Physical Education

This physical education (PE) schedule contains ideas for seven weeks of PE sessions. The schedule can be adapted to fit the needs and abilities of an individual class. Each session should include a warm up and cool down, incorporating basic stretches. Some exercises may require a ball or other basic equipment, and teamwork is needed to perform the partner exercises.

Warm Up Ideas	Cool Down Ideas
Jumping Jacks	Calf Stretch
Shoulder Rolls	Hamstring Stretch
Angle Bounces	Quad Stretch
Arm Circles	Tricep Pull
Heal Raises	Wall Chest Stretch
Upper Body Twist	Arm Cross Pull
Jumping Rope	Butterfly Stretch
Jogging in Place	Cat Stretch
Skip-Hop	Supine Torso Twist
Boxer Shuffle	Toe Touch
Quad Stretch	Downward Dog Stretch
Hamstring Stretch	Cobra Stretch

Set = 10 repetitions

PE Schedule	Monday	Tuesday	Wednesday	Thursday
Week 1	Kick ball	**Pushups** – 1set **Squats** – 2 sets **Swimmers** – 2 sets **Jumping jacks** - 3 sets	Capture the flag	**Partner exercises** (3 sets each) - **Curl ups** - **Leg raises** - **V-sit with passing ball** - **Lunge with chest pass** - **Squats**
Week 2	**Box jumps** – 2 sets **Sit-ups** – 2 sets **Squat jacks** – 2 sets **Sprints** – x5	Dodge ball	**Walking/ Jogging** – ½ mile **Plank** – 15 secs, x2 **Side hip raises** – 2 sets, both sides	Flag football
Week 3	Obstacle course	Relay races	**Partner exercises** (3 sets each) - **Reach & touch plank** - **Split lunge** - **Pushups with high five** - **Medicine ball slam**	Hiking

Week 4	Circuit training (5 rounds) - Skipping - Pushups - Leg raises - Swimmers - Jumping jacks - Mountain climbers	Kick ball	Walking/ jogging – ¾ mile Lunges – 2 sets Side plank – 20 sec, both sides	Ultimate Frisbee
Week 5	Flag football	Partner exercises (3 sets each) - V-sit with passing ball - Medicine ball slam - Team burpees - Single leg chest pass - Curl ups	Light warm up Burpees – 2 sets	Relay sprints Mountain climbers – 2 sets
Week 6	Circuit training (5 rounds) - Jogging - Burpees - Squats - Sit ups - Bicycles - Skipping	Obstacle course	Jump rope – 20 sec, x5 Box jumps – 2 sets Dodge ball	Walking/ jogging – 1 mile Plank – 15 sec, x2
Week 7	Relay races	Walking/ jogging – 1 mile Pushups – 2 sets Squats – 2 sets	3-legged races Cotton ball races	Free day

Spontaneous Devotion

The following is a poem by Al Franklin, the originator of the Outdoor Leadership course. The poem was composed during a quiet time of reflection by a wilderness stream. Set aside time on hikes and camping trips to listen for God's voice, and encourage students to express what they hear in poems, songs, and encouraging words. This poem is an example of creativity inspired by the Holy Spirit in a wilderness setting.

Quiet Moments on Sugar Creek

Watching the creek flow, I wonder
where it's going, I'd like to know.
It ripples and boils for us to see,
Graceful and alluring as God meant it to be.
Rocks and drowned trees are in its way,
To get around, the currents must obey.

As it flows, a gentle noise can be heard,
A gurgling, tinkling sound, almost like a bird.
The creek is moving, cleansing, refreshing,
Bringing new life to the land.
Like the Holy Spirit does for us,
On another plan.

The creek is marching along as though on a mission,
And within its slow winding path,
There might even be some good fishin!

SECTION IV

ABOUT THE AUTHORS

About the Authors

Kari Barr

Kari Barr has taught in Christian Education for twenty-three years. She loves her students: especially helping them understand math in a kingdom atmosphere. Kari has been teaching Algebra the last eighteen years and enjoys ministering to those students who struggle in math so they too can be successful.

Julie Brown

Julie Brown has taught high school English for eighteen years in both public and private schools. She has a passion for people to understand their royal identity in the kingdom of our Lord and of His Christ. Julie and her husband, Jeff, live in Fort Mill, South Carolina.

Joe Chamberlin

Joe Chamberlin met the Lord (and his wife) back in the Jesus Movement of the 1970s. His three careers include the Navy, Safety Engineering, and eighteen years making high school math and science creative and fun. Joe has retired, but continues to teach a stained-glass elective at CSCL.

Michael Fickess

Michael Fickess calls students to pursue an intimate relationship with God through activation and exploration of the "deeper mysteries" of the Word. In addition to teaching Bible for all ages at CSCL, Michael is a prolific author. He and his wife, Rachelle, live in Charlotte, North Carolina, and have two children, Samuel and Ari.

Al Franklin

Al Franklin has spent his life working with students – 50+ years teaching and sharing his love for science exploration and God's awesome creation. Al is married with two children and four grandchildren. He teaches middle school science and the outdoor leadership elective at CSCL.

Ximena Gonzalez

Ximena Andrea Gonzalez Parra (BA in Bilingual Education and Leadership) is from Bogotá Colombia. She desires to cultivate a fierce passion for the Bible, the presence of God, and His heart for the next generation. Ximena is now the Children's Pastor at Soul Church, U.K. and is working toward a Masters in Theology.

Dawn Hartigan

Dawn Hartigan is a painter and an art teacher, currently teaching art to elementary students at CSCL. She enjoys encouraging, training, and mentoring students to pursue their creativity in the arts. Dawn graduated from Syracuse University with a Bachelor of Arts degree in Art Education and Fine Arts.

Erin Hogan

After graduating from CSCL in 2004, Erin Hogan received her B.A. in elementary education from Queens University of Charlotte. After two years in the public schools, Erin taught at CSCL where she spearheaded the recycling program, trained phonics volunteers, and organized field trips. Erin enjoys spending time with her husband and three children, being outdoors, and traveling.

Charlotte Jordaan

Charlotte's passion for teaching and her love for students is evident to all who encounter her. She has been teaching phonics at CSCL since 2013. Charlotte has a doctorate degree in Theology as well as an ESL qualification. Charlotte also trains and releases young worship leaders at the school.

Sheila Lester

Sheila spent twenty-five years as a teacher and vice-principal in public education working extensively in the area of school reform. She is passionate about God's plan for reforming education and building "kingdom" schools. Sheila currently teaches senior Bible, is the Guidance Adviser and the Vice-Principal of Academics at CSCL.

Marcia Rensink

Marcia Rensink loves equipping the next generation with kingdom tools for life. She is a dedicated educator who has taught for over twenty-seven years. She teaches at CSCL, administrates the U.S. office for Lespri Ministries, and serves on healing teams. She and her husband Valiant live in Fort Mill, SC.

Donna Reynolds

Donna Reynolds is a passionate lover of God who enjoys teaching academics and spiritual life lessons to her students. She spent five years at CSCL encouraging her students to seek the presence of the Lord. Donna and her late husband Dave have three children and eleven grandchildren.

Clint Rogers

Clint Rogers began teaching in public schools in Atlanta in 1999 and has been teaching social studies at CSCL since 2006. Clint believes "school" is broken and needs an "evolution." School should be fun and filled with risk-taking, yet with work accomplished and preparation for the world we live in today.

Trace White

Trace White is in his fifth year at CSCL. He teaches leadership and entrepreneurship, but is most passionate about mentoring the next generation to shift the spheres of influence in society. Married to Mia and a father of nine, he is a school planter and advocate of kingdom education.

Sandy Woods

Sandy Woods, principal at CSCL since 2010, believes that equipping today's youth to be resilient followers of Christ who know their purpose lies with kingdom education. She and the staff actively promote the Comenius' philosophy of education to help others start CSCL-type schools.

Comenius School For Creative Leadership (CSCL)

The Comenius School for Creative Leadership (CSCL) located in Fort Mill, South Carolina, began as a home school co-op in 1998 and quickly expanded into a K-12 school. With an emphasis on creativity in the classroom and developing leaders in the school population, the staff aims to raise kingdom minded students who know the Lord, recognize their purpose and use their gifts and talents to influence society. It is their hope to inspire and equip other educators to transform their school to reflect the kingdom. Each year the school receives visitors during its Kingdom Educator Immersion who wish to view firsthand the methods used by the staff and to experience its kingdom culture and spirit filled atmosphere.

KINGDOM
Education

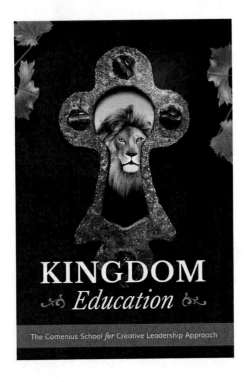

Kingdom Education: The Comenius School for Creative Leadership Approach, the first book written by the CSCL staff, discusses a revolutionary teaching philosophy that balances centuries old principles of learning with modern advancements in culture and technology.